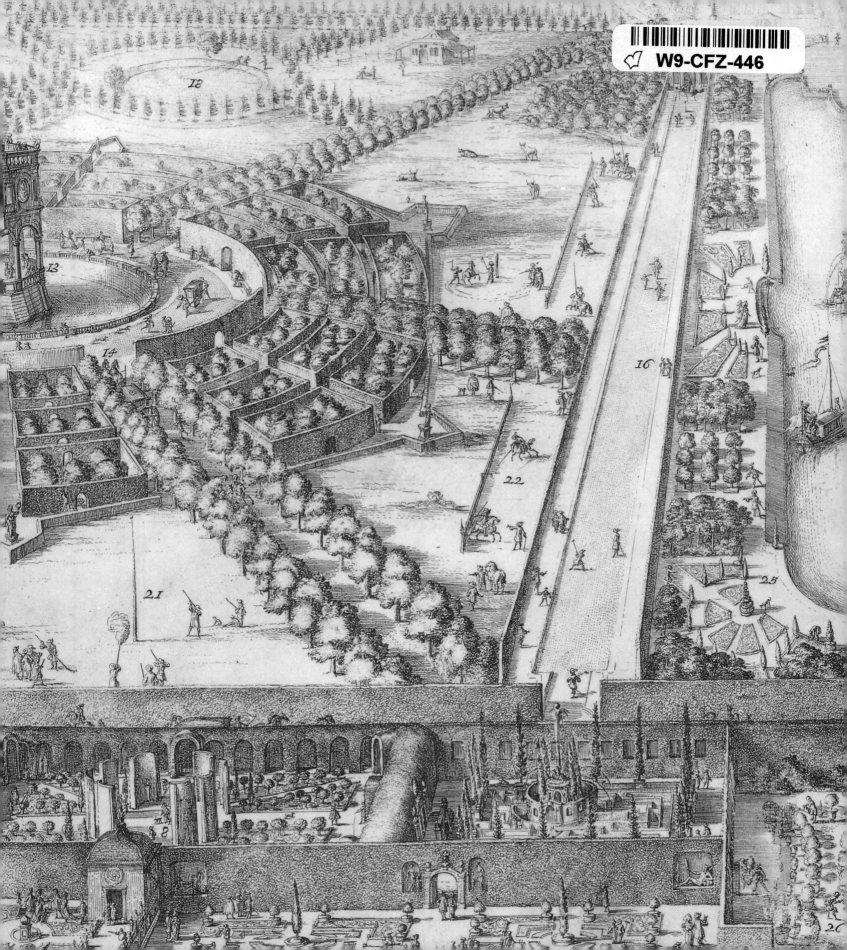

Pleasures of the Garden

MAC GRISWOLD

PLEASURES OF THE GARDEN

Images from The Metropolitan Museum of Art

The Metropolitan Museum of Art, New York

Harry N. Abrams, Inc., Publishers, New York

Frontispiece
Wang Hsi-chih Watching Geese
(detail)
Ch'ien Hsuan,
Chinese, 14th century

A garden is often a place where
artists find inspiration. From his
ting, or pavilion, Wang Hsi-chih,
the same calligrapher who immor-
talized the gathering of poets at the
Orchard Pavilion reproduced on
page 55, watches two geese swimming. From their graceful move-
ments, it is said, he learned the
secrets of beautiful calligraphy, for
which he became famous. This
scene commemorates his source of
inspiration; it was painted almost
one thousand years after his death.

Published by The Metropolitan Museum of Art, New York
Bradford D. Kelleher, Publisher
John P. O'Neill, Editor in Chief
Barbara Burn, Project Supervisor
Homans/Salsgiver, Design

Library of Congress Cataloging-in-Publication Data

Metropolitan Museum of Art (New York, N.Y.)
    Pleasures of the garden.

    1. Gardens in art—Catalogs.   2. Gardens—Design—
Catalogs.   3. Metropolitan Museum of Art (New York, N.Y.)
—Catalogs.   I. Griswold, Mac K.   II. Title.
N8217.G36M4   1987   704.9′436′07401471   86-23628
ISBN 0-87099-481-6
ISBN 0-8109-0997-9 (Abrams)

Typesetting by Trufont Typographers, Inc.
Printed and bound by Dai Nippon Printing Co., Ltd., Tokyo, Japan

CONTENTS

INTRODUCTION

Like a gardener in winter dreaming over seed catalogues, I began this book by looking at pictures, peering into the green or flowery backgrounds of works of art at the Metropolitan Museum. As I imagined my ideal garden, I realized that gardens in art, unlike portraits of flowers, tell a story of how people have hoped their surroundings would look. For gardens have a much greater expressive range than the flowers, trees, shrubs, and vegetables they may include as parts of their design, and people have had deeper and more complicated feelings about them. We take gardens personally, or maybe it would be more accurate to say we regard them as works of art we create and constantly improve. All who garden, and many who do not, fantasize about changing their lives by changing their surroundings. This book will show us the gardens in The Metropolitan Museum of Art, which, quite apart from their beauty, speak movingly to this universal desire.

The history of gardens is a wonderful tangle, not easy to unravel, and those who want more should begin with Christopher Thacker's *The History of Gardens*. Gardens constantly change through growth and neglect: they are determined by climate and must accommodate existing natural features or parts of older designs. After all, gardens themselves do not exist on pieces of paper that can be preserved intact. Works of art present different states of a garden as it evolves over time, and through such images we can follow historical changes in a way that is no longer possible on the ground, so to speak. But to suppose these images are accurate is risky; reasons for depicting gardens have always been diverse, and artists invariably interpret what they see. Just because artists' renderings *are* subjective we can gather from them important information about the history of ideas and the taste of the times. Even the most straightforward topographical print tells us something about what the perfect garden of the period should have looked like. Then, too, from works of art we get an intriguing sense of social history, of the life of the times as it took place in the garden. In these pages you will see a centuries-long parade of games, sports, and quieter pleasures quite unrelated to those of digging in the garden or sniffing the flowers. It is not a book about horticulture, although I have tried—with help from Rupert Barnaby of the New York Botanical Garden, Lawrence Crockett of the City College of New York, Pamela Lord, and others—to identify as many plants as possible.

From the huge number of garden images in the Metropolitan Museum I have chosen many that are "secret gardens" rarely seen by museum visitors. Some are secrets because they are so fragile, like the fan on p. 50, and some, like the lacquer incense box on p. 96, because there has been no permanent exhibition space for them. Other gardens are familiar masterpieces, such as Monet's *Terrace at Saint-Adresse* on p. 115. I am indebted to many members of the Museum's curatorial staff who have answered my questions and led me to their own favorites.

In writing this book I am deeply grateful to Mary Laing, who was an integral and inspiring part of it all from start to finish, smoothing my path throughout the Museum as well as smoothing the bumps out of my prose. I thank Barbara Burn for giving me a chance to write this book and her and her staff for their help and advice. Richard Poirier, Tim Lovejoy, Elizabeth Banks, Leslie Close, and other friends made thoughtful suggestions and comments. To Katy Homans I owe special gratitude for her elegant and sympathetic design. Finally, and most of all, I thank Frederick Seidel for his continuous help, even when I didn't know I needed it, and my wise and forbearing children, Belinda and Anna Brown, who put up with me in the throes of my first book.

CHAPTER ONE

Gardens of Paradise

Peach Blossom Spring
Fan Ch'i,
Chinese, 1646

A fisherman boated along a stream one day and, unconscious of how far he had traveled, was surprised to find a huge grove of peach trees in fragrant flower. At the end of the grove, a spring and a grotto led him to an enchanted country. He left, intending to return, but could never find the way back. So T'ao Ch'ien, the great 5th-century poet, tells the story of *Peach Blossom Spring*—a story that quickly became a favorite of poets and painters and remains an enduring symbol of paradise. Fan Ch'i's album leaf was painted more than a thousand years after T'ao's death. The fisherman's tale echoes the garden experience: suspension of ordinary space and time, except for the passage of the seasons; beauty and fragrance; and seclusion from the world.

Paradise, the word for an idyllic place where human life began, or where—if they are lucky—men and women may end, goes back to the Old Persian for an enclosure or park, just as the homegrown words garden and yard share an Indo-European root, *gher*, meaning some kind of domestic enclosure. So it is not surprising that paradise is invariably imagined as a garden.

Artists have created as many images of paradise as there are kinds of gardens. Every culture and every period has its own version: the Garden of Eden, the Elysian Fields, the Taoist Isles of the Blest, and the Buddhist Pure Land where the faithful achieve enlightenment sitting on the petals of lotus flowers—and where doubters are shut up in their flowers for five hundred years to reflect. The variety of these visions extends the idea of a garden far beyond that of a place to grow flowers; paradise gardens include groves, flower-sprinkled fields, orchards, parks, and even lakes and grottoes. Such garden images, and such gardens, are man's effort to re-create paradise on earth.

The concept of paradise, a perfect world usually unattainable except through death, is a promise made to true believers in most of the world's religions. But because paradise gardens in sacred texts such as the Bible or the Koran are filled with images of earthly beauty, paradise sometimes seems tantalizingly near. Perhaps that glimmer of hope is what inspires men to make paradises on earth, gardens filled with fragrance and almost celestial breezes, gardens like the one that prompted the wonderfully named Hildebert de Laverdin, an 11th-century English bishop, gardener, and poet, to say "O Paradise! thy rival is this place."

All images of paradise share certain characteristics: they portray a world outside time, an eternal spring or a bounty of flowers and fruits of all seasons growing together. The landscape is sure to be the most beautiful the artist could imagine. The flowers and trees, whether realistic or fantastic, are more wonderful than any earthly plants. Evil and sickness, if they do intrude, signal the start of another story—the story of mankind on earth. By way of work the inhabitants of paradise need only tend what has already been so generously provided. Whether they are the "white-haired elders and tufted children" of the classic Chinese tale *Peach Blossom Spring* or the "agreeable and beauteous damsels" in the heavenly gardens of the Koran, dwellers in paradise enjoy many pleasures. They converse, they embrace, they make music, they are in harmony

In the Sixth Paradise
Attributed to Manohar,
Indian, 1597–1598

Illustrating a poem written some
three hundred years earlier, the
artist shows Bahram Gur, the
hero, visiting the Purple Palace in
the Sixth Paradise, where a
winged Persian princess tells him a
story. Paradise, with the pleasures
promised to believers in the
Koran, is shown as a typical Islamic garden. In the upper left
corner a waterwheel turns above a
cistern, flooding the *chadar*, or
water slide. *Chadars* are carved in
patterns that break up the flow of
the water and make it sparkle and
foam. For Islamic gardens, conceived in the desert, water is literally the water of life. A narrow
irrigation canal runs through the
flowery meadow, whose stylized
wildflowers seem to have escaped
from the tiles or carpet in the
gallery behind. Water appears
again in a rectangular reflecting
pool rimmed by sunken beds.
Such beds, when thickly planted
with flowers that grew to pave-
ment level, resembled a carpet. A
banana tree (*Musa sapientum*)
grows next to the cistern, and
cypresses (symbolizing eternity)
echo the pavilion's columns.
Winged attendants make music
and bring refreshments. In the
starry sky, one winged houri is in
flight—perhaps she brings sherbet
made with snow from the mountains.

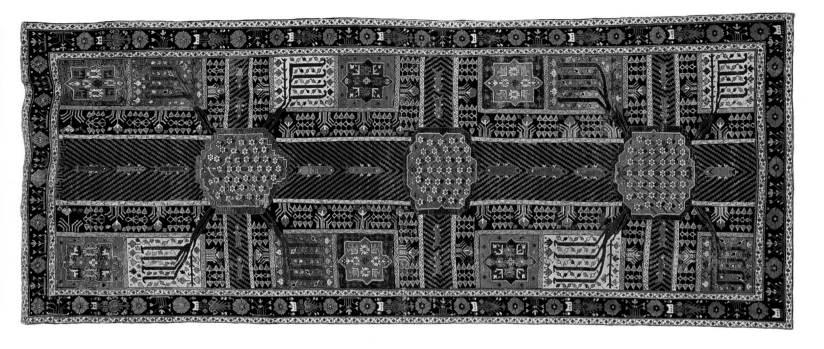

A Carpet Garden
Iranian, c. 1800

The fourfold pattern of Persian gardens is very old: Akkadian kings proclaimed themselves "Kings of the Four Quarters" around 2500 B.C. The crossing of four water courses, here tripled to make a longer carpet, signifies the meeting of the four rivers of life. Pavilions from which viewers enjoy the garden sit atop the crossings, and fish swim in single file in the "streams." The four dark, branching patterns springing from each end pavilion are Oriental plane trees. The rectangular beds are filled with stylized shrubs and flowers. Flowery carpets are often spread in nomad tents as reminders of oasis gardens.

with each other. Even though they may bear the names of gods and goddesses, they are also ourselves as we would like to be.

Images of paradise magnificently offer an explication of the universe, of the cycle of life, death, and rebirth. One of the most touching and direct images of resurrection occurs in an ancient Egyptian funeral practice: a bed was placed in the tomb and on it was traced a silhouette in rich earth of Osiris, god of the dead. Just before the tomb was closed, the silhouette was planted with barley and the earth watered; in the darkness of the following weeks, a green and living figure flourished—an image of the god and of the hopeful dead. Each spring when we garden, or watch new grass come up, there is the same secret promise of hope.

Persia—The First Paradise

For the Persians, as much as for any Western culture, a *paradeiza*, or garden, was a symbol of eternal life. The first paradise garden of which any trace remains is that of Cyrus the Great at Pasargadae, on the Iranian plateau, built in 546 B.C. This garden set the pattern for the water channels and pavilions depicted in Mughal paintings over a thousand years later.

Gardeners will be interested to know that the Iranian plateau enjoys an annual rainfall of two to ten inches, blasting winds, bitter winters, and scorching summers. No wonder water, flowers, fruit, and shade were valued highly. The Arabs adopted the *chaharbagh*, or fourfold garden, when they

Funeral Ceremony in a Temple Garden
Egyptian (copy), c. 1475 B.C.

Both species of tree in this typically formal temple garden bear edible fruit. The date palms (*Phoenix dactylifera*) are lined up by sex, with the males on one side of the garden and fruit-bearing females on the other. The other trees are sycamore figs (*Sycamorus antiquorum*). A canopied funeral barque floats on the lotus-filled pool as libations are poured and burnt offerings made below. The long green staffs of the attendants are papyrus stalks (*Papyrus antiquorum*) with the umbels still attached at the top; they are a symbol of rebirth.

invaded Persia in the 7th century, and they established such gardens in every land they conquered, from Spain to India. In these gardens, which were not intended for strolling, beds were planted with rows of trees, then underplanted with aromatic shrubs and flowers. The colorful pattern and symmetry were enjoyed from raised pavilions. Favorite trees were the *chenar*, or Oriental plane (*Platanus orientalis*), with its cool, silver-backed leaves, and the cypress (*Cupressus sempervirens*), a symbol of immortality. Fruit trees introduced later by the Mongols included pomegranate, sour cherry, and sour orange from Thailand, and peach and apricot from China. One good thing that can be said for Genghis Khan is that his descendants brought the peony to the Near East. Lilies, iris, jasmine yellow and white, roses, and crocus were also planted in the beds of the *chaharbagh*. Narcissus were grown in quantity. Mohammed said, "If you have two loaves of bread, sell one and buy narcissus, for bread is food for the body, while narcissus is food for the soul."

The restless Mongols extended the size of the *chaharbagh*, so that it could be used as a place for both activity and repose. They sowed parts of the garden with trefoil clover, making little fields to remind them of the steppes, and in these they pitched beautiful scarlet pavilions and tents made of silk. The Mughals went still further, living in their gardens and carrying out there the business of state and the administration of justice. Love and the moon and the nightingale also had their place, for paradise, says the Koran, is a place of sensual delights. Babur, first and most engaging of the Mughal emperors, was buried at Kabul in one of the many brilliant gardens he made; his epitaph ends with the line "Paradise is forever Babur Padshah's abode." Although the plantings have been swept away, one huge *chenar*, more than 45 feet around, remains at Kabul. It is said to have been planted by Babur himself. Gardens are a cherished paradox in Islam: a reminder of mortality and a symbol of eternity.

The Western Paradise (detail)
Japanese, c. 1300

Amida Buddha escorts a soul to paradise in this detail of an exquisite *raigo* painting. Growing in the heavenly pond are lotus (*Nelumbium nucifera*), from which the soul will be reborn. The golden shore is made of thousands of bits of gold leaf; a lotus petal floating through the air is silhouetted against the gold. On the dark silk shines a celestial pavilion, which resembles the Phoenix Hall built early in the 11th century at Byōdō-in Temple in Kyoto, where the garden was intended to represent the Western Paradise. Hanging scrolls like this were placed at the bedsides of the dying to give them hope and courage in their ordeal.

Passages to Paradise

In many religions the belief that, when we die, rebirth in another life or another form will follow finds a natural parallel in the life cycle of a garden. Throughout history, temple gardens and graveyards have been designed and planted to suggest a vision of the world to come. In Egypt the temple's green surroundings served as an entrance to the world of the dead. Funerary barques, like the one illustrated opposite, made their symbolic way across the temple pool. Trees in a typical temple garden were formally arranged, and steps led from the temple to the pool itself.

At the very end of the 18th century, when Christians stopped dwelling on the more gruesome aspects of human mortality and when it became necessary to find new places to bury the dead, they, like the Egyptians, made funerary gardens, "rural cemeteries," as they were first called. Dotted with tombs and monuments—Egyptian, Greek, Roman, and Gothic—rural cemeteries were a 19th-century version of a paradise garden.

In Japan, the path to the Western Paradise, or the Pure Land of Amida Buddha, lies through the garden. A long period of civil war ended in 1192 with the destruction of the ancient Heian court, the rise of the military caste to power, and the expansion of the Pure Land Buddhist cult. The worship of Amida Buddha, which demands a less intellectual and strenuous approach, was

The Temptation of Adam and Eve
French, c. 1500

This woodcut, a Bible illustration, might well be called "The Root of All Evil." In the middle of the heavily wooded Garden of Eden stands an elegant three-tiered fountain that pours forth the waters of life. Coiled around the Tree of Knowledge is Satan in the guise of a seductive enchantress. The moment of the Fall seems to have already taken place; Adam and Eve, with downcast looks, hold apples and are equipped with fig leaves. Behind Eve sits an ape, symbol of lust. The stag and the unicorn both symbolize Christ and therefore the Redemption to come; they too hate snakes. So does the little genet, a cousin of the ermine, which stands on the carpet of flowers rather bravely close to Satan's tail.

better suited to the new times than other forms of Buddhism, which stress a lifetime of austerity, prayer, and scholarship.

Two of its most attractive tenets are that we need only call on Buddha once in our lives to gain paradise, and that, at death, he will come to aid us. The dominant image of Pure Land Buddhism is the *raigo*, the coming of Amida to meet the dying soul, who is then transported up to the Western Paradise (always shown as a garden) and reborn in a lotus flower. On his descent and ascent, Buddha is accompanied by the twenty-five boddhisattvas, or sages. Foremost among them are Seshu and Kannon, the latter carrying a lotus pedestal on which to bear the soul away.

Late 13th-century *raigo* paintings, like the one on page 13, are colorful, explicit, and full of movement and narrative detail. In these works we sense the intensity and speed of the Buddha's aid to the dying soul and the deeply personal aspect of the tenet that Buddha appears to each and every believer. These spiritual rescues always take place in a garden. In countless images of the period, the dying are shown with their screens and curtains flung open to their gardens into which the Buddha comes. In some versions, the believer has actually been moved from his deathbed out onto the veranda. In the earthly garden, the season is often autumn or winter; in the paradise garden, which resembles that of an earthly palace, it is eternal spring. Out of the heavenly pond emerge the miraculous lotus flowers from which the soul will be reborn. The many lotus-pond gardens in Japan evoke the paradise garden of the Pure Land cult, which remains the most widespread form of worship in Japan today.

The Garden of Eden

There are probably more depictions of the Garden of Eden than any other sacred garden in the Metropolitan Museum's collections. We see different moments in the story—the Temptation, the Fall, the Expulsion. In these renderings, Eden is never laid out with flower beds or garden architecture, although it sometimes has a fountain. In addition, artists have usually put a fence or paling around Eden. In the Middle Ages, when most pictures of the Garden of Eden were made, the image of a fence was enough to tell the viewer he or she was looking at a garden. Inspiration for the images came from many sources: tales of Near Eastern *paradeizas*, European landscapes of varying climates, and, of course, the language of Genesis.

> *And out of the ground made the Lord God to grow every tree that is pleasant to the sight, and good for food; the tree of life also in the midst of the garden, and the tree of knowledge of good and evil. And a river went out of Eden to water the garden; and from thence it was parted, and became into four heads. And the Lord God took the man, and put him into the garden of Eden to dress it and to keep it.*

*The Expulsion of Adam and Eve
from Paradise*
Giovanni di Paolo,
Italian, c. 1445

The medieval world map, or *map-pamondo*, lies inside the many-colored spheres of the elements and the planets, surrounded by a wide blue band on which the signs of the Zodiac are just visible in gold. The darker blue band encircling the whole is the *primum mobile*, or prime mover, which regulates the movement of all beneath it; beyond lies the empyrean heaven, home of God and the angels. At the top of the map is the Mountain of the Moon, an earthly paradise said to be in Africa and long thought to be the location of the Garden of Eden by medieval theologians and geographers. The four rivers of paradise pour from the mountain's flanks and run all over the world. They appear again as muddy ditches beneath Adam and Eve in the Expulsion scene to the right. This small predella panel also foretells the Redemption: even as God stares fiercely at Adam and Eve, he points to the spot on the Zodiac marking the date of the Annunciation, March 25, a sign of the coming of the light of Christ—and of lengthening spring days. But his gesture seems lost on Adam and Eve as they walk sadly out of Eden across a tapestry of flowers, which includes pinks, ranunculus, lilies, strawberries, and a climbing rose.

Gardens figure in the New as well as the Old Testament. The Passion began with Christ's Agony in the Garden of Gethsemane and ended with his burial in the garden tomb. The Risen Christ was even mistaken for a gardener by Mary Magdalene, who stood at the empty tomb and turned around to answer the voice that asked her why she wept. The Crucifixion also has links with the garden, for, according to medieval legend, the cross was made of wood from the Tree of Life (Adam had taken a sprig with him when he left the Garden of Eden). The end of the story of Christ's sacrifice is the story of man's entry into paradise, a new Eden free of the possibility of sin.

Enclosed Gardens, Wild Glades, and Fields

When Christians tried to recapture paradise in real gardens or in paintings, they based their ideas on two models. One was the *hortus conclusus*, or enclosed garden, taken from the formal Persian garden with walls, fourfold paths, flowering trees, beds of flowers and grass, and a central water supply. Cloister gardens follow the same plan. The *hortus conclusus*, where Mary, the Virgin Mother, is shown with Jesus, became the symbol first of the Incarnation and later of the Immaculate Conception. Mary was also identified with Solomon's

The Annunciation
Follower of Rogier van der
Weyden,
Flemish, 2nd half of 15th century

Medieval gardens often form the
background for paintings of the
Annunciation, since Mary herself
was referred to allegorically as the
hortus conclusus, or enclosed
garden. The garden glimpsed
through the window here has
many features typical of medieval
times. Within the high walls are
turf benches planted with flowers
as well as grass. These benches
were sometimes used for sitting
and sometimes, as here, for raised
beds. Topiary trees, trained into a
characteristic shape known as *es-
trade*, are placed next to the castle
wall. A path divides the flowery
mead, described by Boccaccio as
"of a deep green, spangled with a
thousand different flowers," from
the farther raised bed, which is
divided into sections. In the middle division we see a horizontal
latticelike frame, probably for
growing pinks or carnations, not
unlike the system still used in
commercial greenhouses today.
The single pink (*Dianthus caryophyllus*) was known as the "nail
flower" because it smells like
cloves, which resemble nails; it
was thus a reminder of the Crucifixion.

Modeled on the *hortus conclusus*, the cloister is an earthly paradise from which the world and its dangers are excluded. The peacock, symbol of vanity, cannot enter this garden where humility reigns, so it perches on the roof. A friar stands on the lawn, or *viridarium*, picking lilylike flowers and putting them into a fold of his habit. They will not be much good for arrangements as they have no stems—perhaps he will use them to make oil of lilies. The banded design on the pots and the shape of the tower point to a location in northern Italy. The only available gardeners' guides in the Middle Ages were a few Latin works on horticulture like the one from which this woodcut comes. Such books would have had advice for growing plants in the Italian climate, less useful farther north. In colder cloister gardens, unlike the Garden of Eden, much experimentation must have gone on to determine hardy species.

beloved in the Old Testament *Song of Songs*. There we find the most fragrant, sensuous, enclosed garden of all, one that takes us directly back to a Persian *paradeiza*:

> *A garden enclosed is my sister, my spouse; a spring shut up, a fountain sealed. Thy plants are an orchard of pomegranates, with pleasant fruits, camphire with spikenard. Spikenard and saffron; calamus and cinnamon, with all trees of frankincense; myrrh and aloes, with all the chief spices. A fountain of gardens, a well of living waters, and streams from Lebanon.*

Mary as a garden of secure delight, the earth as a garden of maternal embraces: the image has many variations. Bernaert van Orley's Renaissance Virgin and Child are sitting in a different version of the enclosed garden. In an earlier enclosure, the gate would have been closed; here, it is not clear whether there is a gate at all. A road leads to the meadows and a fanciful landscape beyond. By the 16th century, the European world was seen as a safer, better place to be than it had been in the Middle Ages, and the view outside has become an extension of the paradise garden itself. By contrast, Gauguin's tropical paradise is entirely open; it is the flowering landscape of a Tahitian

Virgin and Child with Angels
Bernaert van Orley,
Flemish, early 16th century

The beautiful gold fountain was not an uncommon feature of Renaissance gardens. However, like many of the details in Flemish paintings, it is also a symbol: here it signifies the Immaculate Conception. A columbine (*Aquilegia vulgaris*), whose lead-purple blossoms are nearly invisible in the shade it loves, grows beside the singing angels. The Latin word *columba* means dove, a symbol of the Holy Spirit. Accurately observed plantain (*Plantago major*), a weed we all try to remove from our own lawns, grows next to the Virgin's fur robe. It indicates the path of the Lord. Other symbolic plants are strawberries (*Fragaria vesca*), a sign of both earthly and heavenly delights, and the little curly rosettes of star-of-Bethlehem (*Ornithogalum umbellatum*). The steps leading up to the patch of green on which Mary sits are an interesting feature new in the Renaissance; changes of level were rare in medieval gardens. A magnificent portico extends from the garden facade, and cobbles on the path and courtyard make the surface easy to walk on in any weather.

village. Enclosure is not needed in a place where nature and man, as Gauguin sees them, are in harmony. The monumental woman in red is Eve in the Garden, Virgin of the Annunciation, and Mary the mother, all at the same time. Less absorbed in her child than earlier Madonnas, she looks out at us as if to draw us into the garden too.

The other model for paradise paintings, and for certain parts of actual gardens, was the *locus amoenus*, the classical Roman "pleasant place" descended from the sacred groves of various deities. The Garden of Eden was based on the *locus amoenus*, an informal array of forest trees and wildflowers.

Ia Orana Maria
Paul Gauguin,
French, 1891

The title in Tahitian dialect means "I hail thee, Mary," the angel Gabriel's first words to the Virgin at the Annunciation. The most important picture Gauguin painted on his first trip to the South Pacific, *Ia Orana Maria* sums up the artist's feelings about having discovered an unspoiled paradise. In 1892 he described the painting to a friend: "An angel with yellow wings who points out to two Tahitian women the figures of Mary and Jesus, also Tahitians. . . . In the background somber mountains and blooming trees. . . . I am rather pleased with it." Any medieval painter or gardener would have understood the scene, despite his unfamiliarity with the frangipani blooming beside the angel Gabriel.

During the Middle Ages, the only "gardens" that looked like this were wild glades that people surely stumbled on in the dark forest, sun-filled grassy openings spangled with flowers that no one had planted or tended. Late Renaissance gardens sometimes had man-made wildernesses, thickets of flowering trees cut through by meandering paths. Medieval romancers used such wild glades as settings for adventure, as in Guillaume de Machaut's 13th-century poem, *The Romance of the Rose*. From the *locus amoenus* also sprang the garden of the Unicorn and the "shaggie hill" of Milton's Eden in *Paradise Lost*.

A pope in red, wearing his triple crown, meets an angel; lovers are reunited under the trees; church dignitaries, friars, and holy women embrace; and two young beauties in elegantly scalloped robes clasp hands. In this most joyful vision of eternity ever painted, the dark turf of the flowery mead springs with lilies (*L. candidum*), violets (*Viola sylvestris? cornuta?*), and pinks (*Dianthus caryophyllus*), while rabbits hop about underfoot.

In the late 18th century Frenchmen visiting Stowe, one of the tourist attractions of England, were impressed by the Elysian Fields, a part of the garden where the Temple of Ancient Virtue stands on a broad lawn next to the stream, called here the river Styx. The first rural cemeteries were built in France, and they were partly modeled on this garden innovation. After 1749 softer contours replaced the straight lines of the garden throughout, and commemorative monuments appeared everywhere, not only in the Elysian Fields.

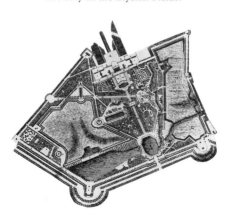

Christian images of paradise as fields owe their inspiration to the *locus amoenus* and to the ancient Greek idea of the Elysian Fields, land of Homer's heroic dead. Fields created by nature and never worked by man, they are made to seem less intimate and more fanciful, more otherworldly than the little medieval enclosed gardens. During the Middle Ages and Renaissance we find many such flower-starred meadows in painting and tapestry. Small square or rectangular lawns, known as "flowery meads," were common features in medieval gardens. Later garden "fields" were bigger and grassier, like the silvery, sheep-cropped sward of the English landscape garden.

By the 18th century, the Fields of Paradise had become wholly secular. English aristocrats looked to classical models when they gave the name Elysian Fields to parts of their landscape gardens. For a visual model, they used Nicolas

Elysian Fields
After Lodovico Burnacini,
German, 1678

In the 16th and 17th centuries,
masques took place in the garden,
and artists produced suites of designs like this one from *La Monarchia Latina Triomfante.*
Burnacini's "Elysian Fields" look
very like a typical formal 17th-
century allée, even though the
artist has added a thick under-
planting of tulips and a sunflower
or two. Beyond are mountains,
descendants of the terrible pointed
medieval rocks that warned of the
world outside the Garden of Eden.

Poussin's and Claude Lorrain's Virgilian visions of pastoral landscape. At Stowe
in Buckinghamshire, the most influential garden of this kind was created in 1739
by Charles Bridgeman and perhaps also by William Kent, who designed
theatrical sets as well as landscapes. Certainly the garden was initially like a set
for a play. Strollers in the "Elysian Fields" became involved in a complicated
political satire about Whigs and Tories worked out in the inscriptions and
symbolism of monuments like the Temple of British Worthies—the new
Elysians. Within ten years, however, most of the intricate political references
were forgotten, and visitors saw the garden simply as an idealized landscape,
truly Virgilian, "a land of joy, the green pleasaunces and happy seats of the
Blissful groves" (*Aeneid*, Book 6).

The Trees of Paradise

Trees play such a prominent part in the stories and pictures of paradise that it is
worth asking why. Their cool shade is always mentioned, of course, as is the
beauty of their blossom and their delicious fruit, but they seem particularly
appropriate to paradise imagery for another reason. Trees are big—bigger than
other plants in the garden and longer lived. Unlike most flowers, they do not
wither and die down every year. Their grand architecture stands comparatively
unchanged in the garden at every season, exemplifying the eternal and the
transient together in a particularly satisfying and striking way. The Greeks had
their sacred groves, which sometimes served as temples without any structure
except an altar. In the 7th century B.C. Sappho invoked Aphrodite:

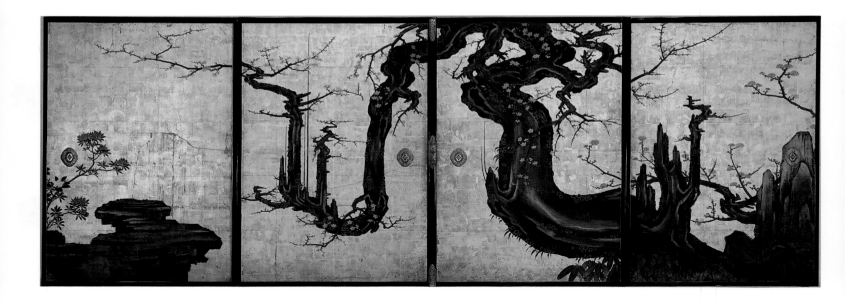

The Old Plum
Attributed to Kano Sansetsu,
Japanese, 1647

The flowering plum (*Prunus mume*) blooms triumphantly on the oldest and most rotten-looking wood. In the garden, in art, in Japanese life itself, the plum is the symbol of fortitude as well as spiritual rebirth, since its fragile white buds impossibly appear in the middle of winter, right after the New Year. Later-blooming azaleas on the left hint at the further passage of the seasons. These sliding panels were probably painted for a reception room in the abbot's residence at the Tenshō-in, built in 1647. When the doors separating the room from the veranda slid open, light from the garden that lay beyond would have bathed the gnarled and ancient trees of this imaginary garden within.

Come to your grove,
Mellow apple trees
And holy altar
Where the sweet smoke
Of libanum is in
Your praise.

Where leaf melody
In the apples
Is a crystal crash,
And the water is cold. . . .
        (tr. Guy Davenport)

It was Aphrodite who won the golden apple from Paris, and the garden of the Hesperides had its golden apples too, well protected by the dragon, Ladon, who lay coiled around the tree trunk. We think of the apple tree (*Malus pumila*) as the tree of the Garden of Eden, perhaps because it has always been the most familiar fruit tree in the West, but the Bible does not tell us so; it says simply "the tree of knowledge of good and evil." Often, indeed, the fruit trees of paradise look more like orange trees, as do the beautiful glossy-leaved specimens in the two paintings by Giovanni di Paolo reproduced in this chapter. The bitter Seville orange (*Citrus aurantium*) was introduced to Europe through Spain by the Moors; it was growing in such suitably warm places as Italy by the 12th century. The highly prized sweet or China orange (*Citrus sinensis*) arrived in the 15th century and in Flanders was known as the Chinese apple. Like trees in paradise images, the orange tree bears fruits and sweet-scented flowers simultaneously and continuously. But apple and orange trees are not the only

Pollinating the Sacred Tree (detail)
Neo-Assyrian, 9th century B.C.

Such trees, symbols of fertility and life, are a common motif in Assyrian art. Although the species has not been identified, it looks like a date palm (*Phoenix dactylifera*), the staff of life in the Ancient Near East. The date palm has been laboriously hand pollinated for centuries by tying bunches of male flowers to clusters of flowers on the female tree. Eagle-headed winged beings and trees like this are repeated on other reliefs from the state apartments of Assurnasirpal II's great palace at Kalhu, the modern Nimrud.

Flowering Apple Tree in Middletown, New Jersey
George Tice,
American, 1981

This exquisite gelatin-silver photograph shows an apple tree flourishing in a neglected pocket of suburbanized nature—a bittersweet paradise regained. "A Paradise with all her Virgin Beauties" is how early promoter Robert Mountgomry described America in 1713. Quickly the land was despoiled, an almost inevitable result of human occupation. As historian Annette Kolodny has said, "Only in America has the entire process remained within historical memory, giving Americans the unique ability to see themselves as the willful exploiters of the very land that had once promised an escape from such necessities."

Child in Forest
Wynn Bullock,
American, 1951

Eden as lost childhood, earth as our mother, and paradise as a maternal "garden" nurturing human children—these are all universal myths. Bullock photographed his daughter Barbara in an environment where he felt that "the human figure, the trees, plants, ferns, and flowers manifest the cyclic forces of life and death." The eerie opening in the forest, with its filtered light falling impartially on the sleeping child and the rotting tree trunk lying next to her, looks like a natural paradise, but one in which we are no longer sure what story is being told.

ones to appear in paintings and descriptions of paradise. There is also the sacred Indian bo-tree (the peepul, or *Ficus religiosa*), beneath which the Buddha sat for many years until he gained perfect enlightenment. In the Persian *paradeiza*, the omnipresent *chenar* is a reminder of the shade-giving Tuba tree in the Koran. For Hindus the holy tree is the huge banyan (*Ficus benghalensis*), with ashy-pale branches that bend down to earth to take root.

A Paradise Within

During the 19th century, exploration of the globe and advances in the natural sciences led to changes in the image of paradise. Christian paradise, an idea already undermined during the increasingly secularized 18th century, disappeared as a serious subject for artists. The vision of an ideal world—an earthly paradise—as garden or field vanished as well and was replaced by pictures of wild or remote landscape. Artists such as Frederic Church and Martin Johnson Heade offered monumental scenes of nature untouched by man as new visions of a paradisiacal world. Gardens in art lost their mythical and religious significance and became everyday settings for plein-air artists to explore color harmonies and for anecdotal painters like James Tissot (p. 116) to capture glimpses of contemporary life.

*Garden of Love
(Improvisation Number 27)*
Wassily Kandinsky,
Russian, 1912

Instead of illustrating religious or mythological stories, modern painters are concerned with the interior gardens of memory and sensation. Kandinsky, who was a gardener himself, created this "garden" during his first year as an abstract painter. The name, *Garden of Love*, trails a cloud of passionate, magical references that begin with Guillaume de Machaut's 13th-century poem *Romance of the Rose* about the first "garden of love," which is perhaps all the more romantic for being only half-remembered. The stained-glass light of Kandinsky's painting keeps alive the spirit of the secret walled garden and the mysterious place in the forest.

Darwin's theory of evolution, with its perception of man's ultimately tiny and transient role in the universe, sapped what power was left in the image of the Garden of Eden. By the early 20th century, the perfect structure of flowers was no longer proof of a benevolent universe. The imposition of garden design on nature could no longer carry the conviction of man's ability to order his surroundings harmoniously. Wild nature, now so quickly disappearing, began to be seen as the remnant of unattainable paradise, as paradise lost. Today, with the exploration of our psychological selves, it may be that the only true paradise left is the image we create in our minds, a new version of Milton's "paradise within." It is an image that nonetheless still seems to have real power to console and delight. Very subjective images in art, very private gardens in life, constitute our efforts to evoke paradise in the world today.

CHAPTER TWO

Parterre, Park & Wilderness

The Bathing Pool
Hubert Robert,
French, 1777

This painting is one of six commissioned for a boudoir in the
château of Bagatelle near Paris,
which was built in sixty-four days
on a bet between its owner, the
comte d'Artois, and Queen Marie-
Antoinette. The delicious lux-
uriance and decay seen here are
what 18th-century French painters
admired in the villa gardens of
Rome and Frascati. Robert's
sketchbook, *Les Soirées de Rome,*
became very popular through engravings and had a great influence
on landscape gardening. For all its
monumental scale, the half-ruined
temple here is a reminder of the
little Temple of the Sibyl at Tivoli
which overlooks the steep fall of
the River Anio; versions of it
ornament scores of 18th-century
European gardens. Despite the air
of seeming neglect, the pots and
the planter in the foreground
blooming with summer flowers
are a reminder that this is a
garden, not a wilderness.

Ornamental gardens are works of art. They are, it is said, most closely related to painting but have parallels also in architecture and music. And indeed gardens *do* closely resemble paintings, with foreground, middle, and background, as well as planned perspectives. Garden designers, like painters, often use framing devices, like the two trees that lean over the water in Hubert Robert's *Bathing Pool.* These compositions depend for their effect on light, shade, and distance.

The architecture of gardens defines and organizes space just as the architecture of buildings does. Italian Renaissance gardens have a structure of alternating open and closed forms with many changes of level. An 18th-century English landscape park is another kind of architecture, a coherent, if irregular, mass whose overall shape is determined by artfully designed hills, woods, and water. Gardens, like buildings, depend on variations of rhythm; their architectural incidents are trees, flowers, or garden structures.

Gardens can also be considered the slowest of the performing arts; their performances, in the happiest cases, unfold over centuries as the trees and other slow-growing parts of the design mature. The seasons are variations on a theme. Like music, gardens also need a certain passage of time in which to be experienced. In most cases, walking speed sets the tempo. A great garden is like an opera requiring the close teamwork of many talents—it is rarely the result of only one person's work.

When we first experience a garden we categorize it as we would paintings, buildings, or music. Perhaps the first definition is determined by size and function: is it a botanical collection, a palace garden, a place to grow cabbages, or a backyard in which to sunbathe? Then we define it by style, both the personal style of the maker and the style of the period. A garden designer's style in any period is measured by his or her successful ability to use available assets to best advantage: topography, soil, climate, light, and suitable plants. Period style is characterized by the changing uses of space, by ornament, and by planting and gardening practices. For example, the trees that stand like sparse feather dusters in 17th- and 18th-century landscape paintings are not an artistic convention, but the result of accurate observation; recent research in England has shown that even park trees were heavily pruned at the time. Limbs were lopped both for looks and for necessity, as animal forage and as fuel.

Italian Garden
John Singer Sargent,
American, undated

Who can conceive what a garden
will look like hundreds of years
after its creation? The work of
time, the fourth dimension in gardens, is among every gardener's
fondest imaginary effects, but
most of us cannot really grasp the
magnitude of change. Here the
once-trim classical statue dissolves
before a mass of deep green shrubbery. Sargent's watercolor supplies
what we miss in early topographical prints: the hot light and black
shade we associate with Italian
gardens. The passage of time has
given us the dense foliage, the
secrecy and mystery that we always hope to find at an Italian
villa.

Garden style has been directly influenced by tastes in the visual arts. For
example, Hubert Robert's paintings inspired garden makers, and he himself
recorded and designed many Rococo gardens in France. Best known of the
gardens he worked on is Marie-Antoinette's "farm," Le Hameau, at Versailles.
The romantic overgrown scene shown here is one he himself might have created.
Alas, like many garden designers, Robert was perhaps better in theory than
practice. The Scots gardener and plantsman Thomas Blaikie, who was employed
at Bagatelle among other places, had this to say in 1779:

> those Gardens are Layd out under the Derections of Mr. Robert one of the
> first Landskape painters in France yet however fine his ideas is upon canvas
> yet upon the ground they are without judgement as it is not astonishing he
> knows nothing of the effects of trees nor there color after a feu years'
> growth.

At different periods in the West, gardens have assumed particular
importance as an art form: in Italy during the 15th and 16th centuries, in France

The Gardens of the Villa Aldobrandini (detail)
Giovanni Battista Falda,
Italian, c. 1665

Renaissance gardens were playful and lighthearted. Here a water trick on the staircase shoots out unexpected jets to tickle the visitor's legs. In May 1645 the writer John Evelyn, England's first serious arboriculturalist, described the garden as one of "incomparable walkes & shady groves, aboundance of rare Fruit, Orangs, Lemons, &c. and the goodly prospect of Rome above all description." Begun in 1598, Cardinal Aldobrandini's villa was the first to have a single commanding view—from the Cardinal's quarters—of the entire layout.

Above right: *The Cortile del Belvedere*
Etienne Dupérac,
French, late 16th century

Bramante's courtyard for Pope Julius II, begun in 1505, is a landmark of garden design: for the first time, a central axis unites the whole, as do connecting stairs to the right, between the parterres and the courtyard below. The Belvedere's principal attraction for visitors was not the greenery but Pope Julius's collection of classical statues housed on the upper level.

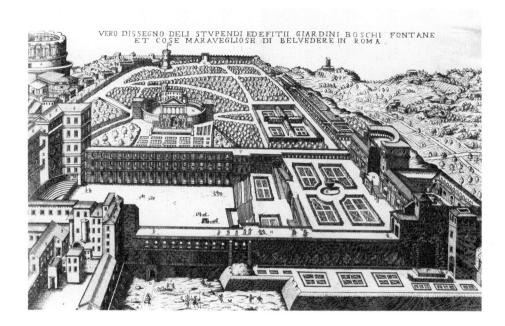

throughout the 17th, and in England during the 18th. The experience of making, enjoying, and discussing gardens became a vital means for people to express their ideas about the world and their place in it. Some of the greatest architects, sculptors, and painters of these epochs worked together with their patrons to create garden masterpieces.

Italian Renaissance Gardens

Renaissance Italians were the first to break out of the medieval enclosure. They saw themselves as the new Romans and made gardens based on the descriptions of Pliny the Younger to accompany their classically inspired villas. Later, their formulations became more original, and gardens were laid out in geometric shapes that harmonized with current architectural forms. The optimism, capacity for play, sensuality, and feeling of world order characteristic of the Renaissance were reflected in gardens of the period. Artists depicted these qualities by showing well-kept gardens bustling with people apparently enjoying the new good times. Doubtless at first these gardens were as bare as those in the Cortile del Belvedere seen here; however, they changed dramatically as they grew. Over time, our perception of Renaissance gardens was altered too, first by the idea of the picturesque and then by the Romantic movement. Two hundred years before John Singer Sargent arrived to paint them, Italian gardens, in art and in life, had already become mysterious and shaggy places, the haunt of solitary visitors.

Plan of the Château of Montargis and Its Gardens
Jacques Androuet du Cerceau,
French, 1607

In late 16th-century France, some old châteaus were still fortified and their gardens were laid out beyond the walls. Here a moat divides the extensive encircling gardens and mazes, with their orderly plantings, from the château's irregular complex of buildings. Du Cerceau's book, *Le Premier Volume des plus excellents bastiments de France*, is a good source of visual information about gardens of this transitional period.

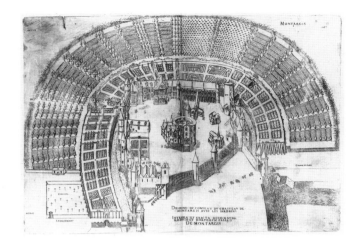

A Town Garden
Joseph Furttenbach,
German, 1640

In this rare picture of a rich burgher's residence in Augsburg, the north side of the house opens into the garden. In the central, ornamental part, a curvy Italianate parterre has taken the place of old-fashioned rectangular raised beds that the kitchen garden at the far end retains. The garden's central axis parallels the house, linking all three parts. At this end is a paved or cobbled working area with a shed.

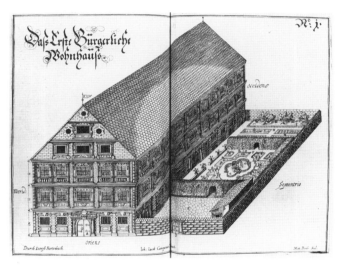

Rubens's House and Garden
Franz Harrewijn,
Flemish, 1692

Few artists have achieved such worldly success in their lifetimes as Peter Paul Rubens. This print, dated some fifty years after his death in 1640, shows the garden facade of his princely Italianate mansion in Antwerp. Formal gardens in the Low Countries were smaller in scale than French ones. Beyond the parterre lies an area carpeted in grass, perhaps for playing games, with a wonderful trellis gazebo. Trellis, that now-vanished art, was once an important garden element.

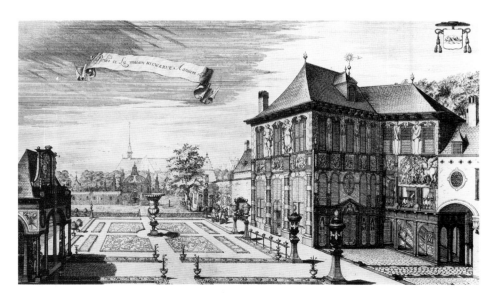

The Huis ten Bosch
Jan van der Heyden,
Dutch, 1668

When the land is flat, pattern is
often a substitute for change of
levels. In this garden of the suburban villa, "House in the Wood,"
at The Hague, the intricate design
of the parterres is intended to be
seen from above, whether from
the house windows, as here, or
from pergolas elevated on mounds
raised in the garden itself. No
trees block the view, though statues and tall trellis poles wreathed
with vines add important vertical
notes. The Dutch were masters of
topiary, but here the bottom of
the undulating hedge looks as thin
as that of many a badly trimmed
modern one. On the grass outside
the parterre, "ruined" pieces of
statuary, reminders of this
garden's Italian heritage, sit cheek
by jowl with two brightly dressed
gardeners who are taking a break.

The Italian Renaissance garden went north to France with a small band of
artists who accompanied the French king Charles VII home from his Italian
conquest in 1495. From France its influence spread throughout Northern
Europe. In the relatively flat countryside the multiple cascades possible in hilly
Italy were smoothed out into canals and glassy basins. In lieu of gravity, the
French and the Dutch developed complex mechanical devices, and the "water
engineer" became easily as important in the garden as the gardener or sculptor.
It is impossible to overestimate the importance of elaborate fountains, jets, and
sprays in such horizontal landscapes. The series of small gardens strung along a
central axis running up and down the hills of Italy became in the north a long
vista of parterres embroidered with flowers and box hedges. To make the
parterre pattern, different-colored pebbles or crushed brick were sometimes
used instead of flowers. Vistas were framed by wedges of woodland, known as
bosquets, which afforded a cool, dark change from the ubiquitous pattern and
open space of the parterres. From these 16th-century bosquets would grow 17th-
century "wildernesses"—slightly larger versions of the same thing, filled with
twisted paths and surprises—and, eventually, 18th-century landscape gardens.

*The Château and Gardens
of Chanteloup*
Louis-Nicolas van Blarenburghe,
French, 1767

This tiny painting on a gold
snuffbox tells us about the Carte-
sian clarity of thought so magnificently visible in French formal
gardens. What other large gardens
in the world could be reduced to
these dimensions and still be com-
prehensible? Grasped at a glance
are the central parterre stretching
in front of the château, the wonderful alternation of greens with
pale yellow sand, and the central
basin with its spritely ascendant
jet d'eau. The elegant château rises
above a unifying system of order,
the vast network of rides cut
through forests to the horizon,
symbol of infinity. Walking in
these immense unshaded gardens
could be hot and tiring (court
diarist Saint-Simon often com-
plained about Louis XIV's inter-
minable progresses along the
allées of Versailles). Only a few
years after this snuffbox was
painted, its owner, the duc de
Choiseul, replaced the hundred-
year-old garden with a *jardin anglais* in the landscape-park style
that swept the French aristocracy
off their feet in the late 18th
century. A magnificent 120-foot-
tall pagoda, very like one in
London's Kew Gardens, and a 17-
acre lake still exist today.

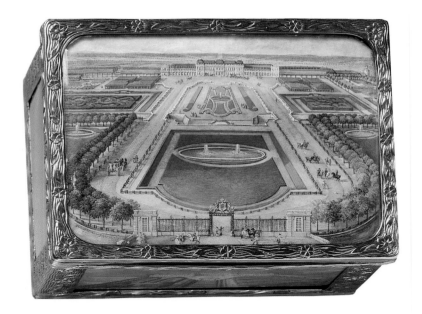

French Formal Gardens

No single garden influenced European garden design as much as that at
Versailles, designed in the 17th century by André Lenôtre for Louis XIV, the Sun
King. Such formal gardens were only one element in an overall artistic program
intended to glorify centralized power, and from then on, every king had to have
a little Versailles, as did every great lord. But even as Western Europe scrambled
to keep up with Louis XIV, the first naturalistic gardens began to appear. André
Lenôtre himself, master architect of the formal garden, may be credited with an
early version. At Versailles in 1675 he laid out the Bosquet of the Springs, a
natural grove of forest trees threaded with streams. By 1685 it had been buried
beneath the stony white curve of the Colonnade built by Jules Hardouin-
Mansard, the royal architect. When the king asked his garden designer what he
thought of the change, the usually affable Lenôtre answered, "Well, Sire, what
do you wish me to say? Of a mason you have made a gardener; he has given
you an example of his métier." The next year, at the age of eighty-one, Lenôtre
built another informal Bosquet of the Springs right behind the Grand Trianon.
Previously he had leveled all trees near buildings, but this time he used the grand
forest trees that stood on the site. This garden was greatly admired. Lenôtre
himself loved it: "I can say it is the one garden, either here or at the Tuileries,
that is pleasant to walk in as well as very beautiful. I can leave the others their
grandeur—this is the most pleasant."

*The Garden at Wilton
Laid Out by Isaac de Caus*
French, c. 1640

This garden might have been invented to illustrate the difference between French and English design philosophy. Wilton, near Salisbury, seat of the earl of Pembroke, had one of the greatest formal gardens in England, 1,000 feet long and 400 wide. It was very elaborate; clearly no expense was spared. Yet the Nadder River runs irregularly across it, something that would have been intolerable in France. In 1896, the garden writer Alicia Amherst said of prints like this: "Faithful representations though they may be in many cases, the formal garden, as they show it, has lost all its poetry; the pale tints of the tender shoots of the beech hedge in spring; the soft green of the sheltering yews in winter, the secluded alley, or the woodbine-covered arbour, have no charm when set down in these stiff lines of black and white."

A Musical Garden Party
British, 1650–1675

The park, or "wilderness," beyond the garden proper began to lose its wildness in the late 17th century. This embroidered picture shows two male singers, gathered with their accompanists on lute, pochette, and flute, *outside* the garden. Behind them, the parterre garden stretches in tilted perspective, planted with tulips, daffodils, roses, carnations, foxgloves, primulas, and canterbury bells. A pavilion wreathed in grapes and clematis looks over both the garden and a view. What a party— Cupid flies through the air accompanying the Spirit of Music!

English Landscape Gardens

Despite such French antecedents, the 18th-century landscape garden is undeniably English. It owes much to a soft climate, a long growing season, and abundant rainfall. Among the landed gentry were many gifted amateurs with taste, imagination, and money who, for more than one hundred years (roughly 1700 to 1825), worked with architects, artists, men of letters, and gardeners, "calling in the country," as the poet Alexander Pope put it, to their enchanting landscapes. The essayist Joseph Addison, the philosopher Lord Shaftesbury, and Pope all wrote about gardens, popularizing a philosophy based on John Locke's theory that reality exists in the viewer as well as in the object viewed. Garden features were therefore designed to arouse differing reactions: exhilaration, melancholy, awe, and contentment. English recognition of individual political liberty was closely related to this notion of individual response. In earlier Italian and French garden plans, ornament had been part of an iconographic program, but 18th-century English Rococo schemes of ornament were connected by the eye and the emotions of the beholder.

The influence of landscape painting on English garden design was strong,
beginning with Claude Lorrain's and Nicolas Poussin's elegiac pastorals of the
Italian countryside based on the poetry of Virgil. English connoisseurs loved
Claude's works (there are more of his paintings in England than anywhere else)
and shaped their properties to match them. The rounded hills, the clumps of
trees, the half-seen house framed by feathery foliage, and above all the merging
of garden into landscape are the hallmarks of English gardens in the mid-18th
century. But by 1790 English painters were recording their own wildest
mountain scenery, and gardeners built rocky mountains right outside the front
door. From the Beautiful and the Sublime (Edmund Burke's distinctions of 1757)
tastemakers proceeded to the shaggier gardens of the Picturesque. By 1816,
when Thomas Love Peacock wrote his satire *Headlong Hall*, the end of the
English landscape movement was in sight. Mr. Gall and Mr. Milestone,
associated respectively with Richard Payne Knight and Humphrey Repton, the
landscape designer, walk around Squire Headlong's grounds:

> *"Allow me," said Mr. Gall. "I distinguish the picturesque and the
> beautiful, and I add to them, in the laying out of grounds, a third and
> distinct character, which I call* unexpectedness."
> *"Pray, Sir," said Mr. Milestone, "by what name do you distinguish this
> character, when a person walks round the grounds for the second time?"*
> *Mr. Gall bit his lips, and inwardly vowed to revenge himself on
> Milestone, by cutting up his next publication.*

But before the landscape passion vanished, the gardens of England had
been transformed by the great mid-18th-century landscape architect Launcelot

Blenheim as Backdrop
British, 1794

Behind this pert fashion model we see Blenheim Palace, John Vanbrugh's honey-colored pile designed for the duke of Marlborough and begun in 1705. Vanbrugh's massive triple-arched bridge spans the lake, Capability Brown's masterstroke in his biggest and boldest landscape. Before Brown dammed the river Glyme, it was an insignificant trickle hardly worthy of the bridge. The Reverend William Gilpin, that great popularizer of the picturesque, said of this view: "The whole of this scenery (the castle, the lawn, the woods, and the lake) seen together, makes one of the grandest bursts, which art perhaps ever displayed." Thomas Jefferson visited in 1786 and reported the landscape park's vast size (2,500 acres), its staff (200 men), and the daunting news that lawns were mowed *every ten days*. Blenheim was such a national landmark the publisher felt no need to identify it in the description of this plate.

Map of Bayham
Humphrey Repton,
British, 1803

Throughout the late 18th century, landscape gardens like this were created all over England, following Capability Brown's lead. Every feature of the landscape had to be "improved": hills were cut and filled, woods felled and replanted, roads changed, rivers dammed or rerouted, and houses pulled down, transformed, rebuilt. All that is missing from the plan for Bayham is the wholesale relocation of a village and its inhabitants for the sake of the landscape "picture." However, by the time Repton made this drawing in 1800, the era of such enormous endeavors was almost over, and in fact the new mansion at Bayham Abbey was never built.

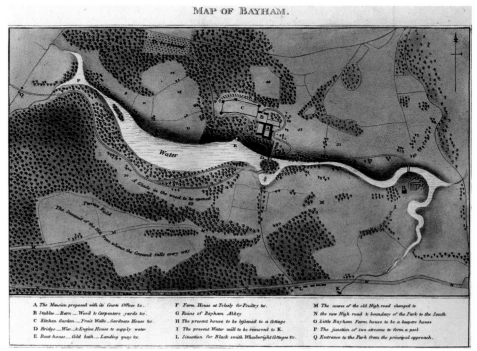

MAP OF BAYHAM.

A The Mansion proposed with its Courts Offices &c.
B Stables — Barn — Wood & Carpenters yards &c.
C Kitchen Garden — Fruit Walls — Gardners House &c.
D Bridge — War — & Engine House to supply water
E Boat house — Cold bath — Landing quay &c.
F Farm House at Tolesly for Poultry &c.
G Ruins of Bayham Abbey
H The present house to be lessened to a Cottage
I The present Water mill to be removed to K.
L Situation for Black smith Wheelwright Cottages &c.
M The course of the old High road changed to
N the new High road & boundary of the Park to the South
O Little Bayham Farm house to be a keeper house
P The junction of two streams to form a pool
Q Entrance to the Park from the principal approach.

*A Repton Improvement
(Page from a "Red Book")*
Humphrey Repton,
British, 1794

In his "Red Books" Repton illustrated the "before" and "after" of
his clients' places. With the flap
down, its present dismal state was
visible; when lifted, it revealed a
pretty picture of the proposed
alterations—here, the conversion
of an avenue into clumps of trees.
Repton's practical suggestions
could be engagingly foolish: he
told one client to stock his lawns
with Alderney cows because,
smaller than other breeds, they
would make the stretch of land
down to the Thames look longer.

"Capability" Brown. Even if we have not seen Brown's gardens, his style is
familiar. The most common image of a park today is a version of a Brownian
landscape garden, the model for many 19th-century public parks in America and
Europe. Big lawns with clumps of trees, irregular lakes with smooth, curved
banks, and perimeter walks with belts of more trees to obscure the boundary
are all features Brown made popular.

He earned his nickname from his habit of saying that a landscape had
"capabilities" of improvement. His own great capability was to discern the
natural character of a site and to use the luxuriant grass and trees of England
liberally and simply. It is said that he had a literary rather than a visual
imagination and the qualities his landscapes lack are visual ones: texture, color,
contrast. His gardens were made according to an almost unvarying formula:
sweeping away the walls and terraces that surrounded country houses and
chopping down the formal avenues of trees planted by previous generations, he
turned all into lawn. Not everyone appreciated the Brownian park:

> *Oft when I've seen some lonely mansion stand*
> *Fresh from th' improvers desolating hand,*
> *'Midst shaven lawns that far around it creep*
> *In one eternal undulating sweep.*
> *from* Richard Payne Knight, *The Landscape: A Didactic Poem*

Humphrey Repton, who was Brown's defender and succeeded to his
aristocratic clientele, nonetheless ended by restoring many formal gardens and
terraces, for convenience and comfort as much as for looks. Repton's changing
ideas over his thirty-year career (1788–1818) parallel developments in garden
design as it progressed from Claudian landscape to the 19th-century garden,
with its emphasis on horticulture. The map of Bayham seen here shows a
Brownian park, but by 1814 Repton was advocating a variety of "trim gardens":
fifteen different kinds of garden enclosure appear on a plan for one eight-acre
site.

From the Sublime to the Gardenesque

After the Napoleonic Wars, agricultural recession, inflation, and the effects of
income tax left few landowners with the means to finance major landscapes.
The new middle class wanted a different sort of garden, scaled down to match
the suburban villa, with affordable comforts and conveniences. The last of the
great gardens—Fonthill in England, Méréville in France—comprised thousands
of acres. But unlike Brown with his carefully edited version of the English
agricultural countryside, their owners, William Beckford and Jean-Joseph de
Laborde, sought to make landscapes that encompassed *all* nature, with an
emphasis on its untamable grandeur. The 18th-century idea of a benevolent

A Rostral Column at Méréville
After Constant Bourgeois,
French, 1808

Just before the French Revolution,
Jean-Josèphe, duc de Laborde,
called on Hubert Robert and architect François-Joseph Belanger
to help shape colossal landscape
pictures of eternal "wild nature"
on a 9,000-acre wilderness tract.
For once, the highest pitch of
romantic sensibility was matched
by the scope of the garden; Laborde was one of the few owners
with the means to create the landscape of his imagination. A dark
blue marble column commemorates two of the duke's sons who
perished on a voyage of discovery
in the South Seas. Exotic trees
were planted around it to evoke
far-off lands (although what the
engraving actually shows is a
weeping willow and a poplar).

creation was becoming untenable: science and exploration kept sending back
reports to the contrary. Nature was more savage than the Scottish Highlands,
and lonelier too.

For related reasons, we find the crowds thinning in garden images.
Paintings and engravings from the Renaissance through the 17th century show
the walks peppered with people, and we know from endless accounts how many
elaborate balls, masques, and fetes took place in gardens. Over the course of the
18th century, we see fewer strollers in garden pictures, and the festivities become
smaller and more informal. By the end of the century, figures are solitary or
nonexistent. The beholder of the image becomes the only presence, alone with
nature as in Delacroix's painting of George Sand's garden.

Disillusionment with the French Revolution made the idea of political
liberty as hard to deal with as the new conception of nature. Garden designers
ceased to feel the need to exemplify liberty or other philosophical notions in
their works. Battles about the picturesque had exhausted tastemakers and left
the general public confused. Almost with relief, everyone decided the garden no
longer had to be a work of art that spoke volumes about things other than
flowers, trees, and shrubs.

"The scenery of nature, called landscape, and that of a garden, are as
different as their uses: one is to please the eye, the other is for the comfort and
occupation of man." This was Repton's view in later life, and it was taken up by
John Claudius Loudon, whose *Encyclopaedia of Gardening* (1822) was the
gospel of a new style, the "gardenesque." Gardens were now supposed to look
like the handiwork of man, not nature. Loudon, whose social conscience was
far in advance of his time, gave advice even the most modest gardener could
follow, and in his publications included plans for small and simple gardens as
well as grand ones. Different flowers and unusual shrubs created a variety of
atmosphere and an illusion of space, ushering in the type of private garden we
are most familiar with today. In a Loudon garden, however, much more than in
a contemporary one, pattern and ornament were everywhere, from the curlicued
flower beds to the wealth of strangely shaped and colored plants from all over
the world. In the mid- and late 19th century, the riches of nature rather than its
wilderness or tranquillity were admired in the garden.

Italianate Gardens in England

In Europe, versions of the landscape garden prevailed until after the mid-19th
century, but in England, starting in the 1840s, architects and designers like
Charles Barry and William Eden Nesfield created Italianate gardens: geometric
ensembles of terraces, steps, urns, jets of water, and precisely laid-out beds in
blocks of bright color. Ironically, these replaced the terraces swept away by
Brown and his school. Such gardens were incredibly labor-intensive, requiring
changes of potted and forced flowers in every season. It is hard to imagine how

*George Sand's Garden
at Nohant*
Eugène Delacroix,
French, 1848

This green garden is empty, but
the sound of Chopin fills the air.
The painting, once George Sand's,
dates from one of Delacroix's
summer visits to her country
house in central France. A fellow
guest wrote of the long pleasant
days, when Delacroix set up his
easel in the garden and Chopin
himself played. This garden is
typically mid-19th century in its
lush, varied planting and its intimacy, though nowhere else at the
time would we have found such a
trio of romantic inhabitants.

wonderful they must have been, since surviving examples are hard and graceless
without proper maintenance and masses of flowers. A glance through the trellis
window of Trentham Hall (p. 6) gives an idea of their vanished charm.

By the 1870s reaction to landscape parks was in full swing. Open spaces,
lawn and gravel alike, were spotted with carpet bedding, unfortunate child of
the gardenesque. Those flat, bright arrangements of dwarf foliage and annuals
we still see rimming the shrubberies and flagpoles of public parks are a legacy
from the day when the well-wrought carpet bed, changing with the season, was
the gardener's pride.

America: Gardens in the Wilderness

Wildness had never been admired in American gardens, though certainly the
wilderness was perceived as sublime. Indeed, a unique American phenomenon
was the revival meeting in virgin forests, where, for a century from the 1730s to
the 1830s, God came to man in lightninglike conversions. But the tremendous

The Camp Meeting
Worthington Whittredge,
American, 1874

By the time Whittredge's re-
vivalists met so tranquilly in the
grove, religious sensationalism
had greatly moderated, but the
grandeur of the landscape per-
sisted. The sense of timeless, almost formless space, so much a
part of the American experience,
would not find its place in gardens
until the 1880s, when Danish immigrant Jens Jensen began to design parks and gardens in the
"prairie style."

Baltimore Sampler
Mary Davis,
American, 1826

The mourning woman, the urn,
and the weeping willow are picturesque elements that could have
been found in many 18th-century
English landscape-garden images.
The little "basket of flowers," a
flower bed with a lattice fence, is a
19th-century development. Symmetry, straight paths, and prim
fences, however, had disappeared
from stylish English gardens by
this date and illustrate the conser-
vatism of American gardeners. A
mixture like this one of farmyard
and flowers was characteristic of
many contemporary American
gardens.

pressure of an untamed forest nearby was something Europeans had forgotten
centuries before. From the moment the first settlers arrived, the wilderness was
an antagonist to be cut down.

The pleasure of a garden is often its very distinction from the world
outside. Highly structured gardens provided welcome relief. Until well into the
19th century, many American gardens were laid out in late 17th-century formal
styles, with an occasional bow to the picturesque. A few rich and secure
seaboard landowners, mostly in the north, created versions of the landscape
garden in the early years of the Republic. By the 1840s Alexander Jackson
Downing, America's first native landscape architect, was enthusiastically
preaching Loudon's theory of the gardenesque, a theory his audience found
more congenial than the picturesque.

The tight curves, narrow vistas, and a specimen tree with variegated foliage are all typical of the *jardin anglais*, or English landscape style, as it developed in Europe in the 19th century. The small scale and sense of control, however, tell us that in fact we are far away from an English landscape park.

Rustic Bridge
Attributed to Henry White,
British, late 19th century

In this photograph a gentleman in his bowler hat crouches meditatively by the stream, and on the hill behind him we can just make out the roofline of a house. In the great rush of carpet bedding and geometric gardens, it is easy to forget how much the Victorians loved the wild outdoors and to what wonderful excesses, like this bridge, the rustic cottage movement of the 1830s led.

From William Robinson to Earthworks

The idea that plants should be grown for their beauty and individuality, not just as blocks of color, took time to develop. By 1829 in England, the distinction was already made between beds composed of just one kind of flower and mixed borders, with plants "arranged so that they may blend with one another in colour as well as in stature," as one innovative garden manual put it.

The pioneer chiefly responsible for this shift in taste was the plantsman and designer William Robinson. Robinson hated the prevailing English Italianate style, and in Paris in 1867 he was struck by French borders planted with a mixture of annuals and "permanent things—lilac bushes, roses, etc. which give a line of verdure throughout the centre of the border, and prevent it from being quite overdone with flowers." In England he combined his love of wild flowers with this new border style and popularized what he termed the "wild garden."

By the 1890s, a new style of English garden had emerged, influenced both by Robinson and by the Arts and Crafts Movement with its stress on England's medieval heritage and on the use of regional materials and local skills. The greatest exponent of this new style was landscape gardener Gertrude Jekyll, who for thirty years worked in partnership with the architect Edwin Lutyens. They met in 1889, as Lutyens said, "at a tea-table, the silver kettle and the

Garden at Vaucresson
Edouard Vuillard,
French, 1923–1937

Vuillard's neighbor, the art dealer
Joseph Hessel, acquired his house
and garden in exchange for a
painting by Cézanne. The feeling
of two-dimensional space bor-
rowed from Japanese prints by
Vuillard, Pierre Bonnard, and
other artists of the period is em-
phasized by the flattened patterns of a lush tangle of flowers.
Through them we peer at a simple
domestic garden that resembles
gardens of today: a double border
of lavender or santolina and roses,
an informal lawn edged by shrubs,
including the cheerful yellow
Scotch broom in flower, and a
cutting or kitchen garden behind
the woman in pink, probably Lu-
cie Hessel.

conversation reflecting rhododendrons." She pioneered the planting of old-
fashioned species perennials with wild flowers and new hybrids, while he
provided the strong architectural framework her billowing flowers needed;
together they established in the garden a closer relationship between indoor and
outdoor space. Gertrude Jekyll's two main assets were her poor sight and her
restraint. Myopia caused her to value the close-up view, the details of flower
and leaf she had learned to love from the practice of embroidery and other
crafts, while her blurry long-range vision increased her perception of light and

Garden of the Aviator
Paul Vera,
French, 1919

masses of color. As for restraint, it was much needed in Edwardian gardens
because, after three centuries of plant introductions and hybridizing, there were
too many plants to choose from. "One modern French artist has described
painting as *l'art des sacrifices,*" Jekyll said, adding that "the best free gardening
is also an art demanding constant restraint and a constant sacrifice."

The English Arts and Crafts garden was not the only historical revival style
to become fashionable early in the 20th century. In America, Charles Platt
revitalized the Italian Renaissance garden. In France, inspired by Lenôtre, the
brothers Vera—André the garden designer and Paul the artist—created a
Cubist-style garden close to other arts of the period. André Vera wrote: "As
painters do not try to create the illusion of real volume in objects, now
landscape architects are not trying to create the illusion of space." The Veras'
gardens are concerned with spatial effects, not with plants. Twentieth-century
art and French garden design came marvelously together at the Paris Exposition
of 1925, in a garden by Robert Mallet-Stevens that featured concrete trees (real
topiary trees of the right size and price were not available when needed). A
British report of the Paris Expo naturally gave these strange, imaginative
stopgaps a brief but nasty mention.

Modern garden design is not often a vehicle for ideas, though the
earthworks of American artists like Walter De Maria, Robert Smithson, Nancy
Holt, and Michael Heiser have certainly made us think about the connection
between wild nature and landscapes as works of art. For now, however, our
own gardens are likely to be retreats designed for privacy, ease, and pleasure,
places, in John Evelyn's words, "Of Verdures, Perennial Greens, and Perpetual
Springs."

CHAPTER THREE

Perennial Pleasures

Everyone is familiar with Robert Herrick's lines: "Gather ye rosebuds while ye
may, / Old Time is still a-flying: / And this same flower that smiles to-day / To-
morrow will be dying." But flowers do spring up each year and garden delights
can be repeated; they are perennial pleasures.

Gardens have been the setting for many pastimes that have little to do with
horticulture, though much to do with the light, air, and space that for centuries
existed in the garden more abundantly than indoors. Such pastimes range from
fantastically imaginative fetes at which thousands of people enjoyed specially
commissioned music, ballets, and plays to the sweetness of drawing a breath
alone in a simple green garden.

The orchard is probably the ancestor of the pleasure ground in the West,
just as the vegetable plot is a forerunner of the flower garden. The Latin word
viridarium is the ancestor of the modern French *verger*, meaning orchard. In the
Middle Ages *viridarium* denoted not a working orchard but a pleasure garden
whose main feature was a lawn surrounded by trees and flowers. In about 1260,
Albertus Magnus, doctor of the Church and the leading scholar of his day,
wrote in his treatise *Of Vegetables and Plants:*

> *There are, however, some places of no great utility or fruitfulness but
> designed for pleasure. . . . mainly for the delight of two senses, viz sight
> and smell. They are therefore provided rather by removing what especially
> requires cultivation; for the sight is in no way so pleasantly refreshed as by
> fine and close grass kept short. . . . Upon the lawn too, against the heat of
> the sun, trees should be planted or vines trained.*

But neither trees nor vines should be planted in the middle of the lawn,
Albertus warns, because "spiders' webs stretched from branch to branch would
interrupt and entangle the faces of the passers-by." Grapevines, pears, apples,
pomegranates, sweet bay trees, and cypresses—trees and vines with perfumed
flowers and agreeable shade—are his choices. A turf bench, flowers, a fountain
of water in a stone basin, herbs for health, and "a free current of air along with
the shade" complete the picture.

Keyboard artists must occasionally have lost their places in the music, imagining themselves in this perfect pleasure garden painted on the inside lid of a double virginal. The garden is big enough for entertainment and active play, as well as for quieter pleasures, and its design accommodates everything from boating to bowls. The sounds of voice, lute, and shawm (ancestor of the oboe) are heard. A feast is spread in the pergola, fragrant with hundreds of red roses, and lovers nestled on the steps lay down their instruments to watch the dancers. Behind the pergola and the arbor is a walled deer park, a common appendage to a nobleman's garden.

From these little *viridaria* sprang the elaborate early pleasure grounds of Northern Europe. Unlike gardens in the Far East, which were seen primarily as retreats, these were showcases designed to display people to their best advantage as they met, played, paired, and enjoyed each other's company in the welcome green freshness. Of course, part of the fun was getting away from the others, into the dark secret arbors concealed in the "wilderness" and behind the high hedges.

Active Pleasures

The active entertainments and sporting pleasures that we enjoy in the garden shape it as much as the use of new plants or the vagaries of style. In 17th-century France, walking was something of a spectator sport, and the wide straight allées of Versailles allowed plenty of room for groups of courtiers to promenade slowly and give each other the once-over. In England, walking has always been considered a pleasure in itself, and by the 18th century the circuit walk had developed from which the whole landscape could be seen in a carefully arranged succession of garden views.

The old sport of hunting stag and boar also influenced garden design. Diagonal paths radiating from a central point had been cut out of the medieval

Party in the Garden of a Castle
(detail)
After David Vinckeboons,
Flemish, 1604?

Vinckeboons's pair of dancers are
earthy yet eerie, their luminous
pallor silhouetted against deeply
crosshatched leafy shade. In the
background we can see four couples dancing in a ring on a green.
During the Renaissance, such
dancing outdoors was a common
pastime. The dances they enjoy
here—perhaps a *galliard, branle*
(the English called it a brawl), or
courante (from the French *courir*,
to run)—were very energetic, and
the place set aside as a dancing
green in the garden had to be big
enough to accommodate them.

"The Pleasures of the Enchanted Isle," one of Louis XIV's first great garden fetes, lasted four days. Temporary stages and proscenium arches like this were set up in different parts of the gardens. The trees of the allée serve as walls, while the distant château itself forms a breathtaking set. A few years later Lenôtre and other artists would build more permanent installations in the bosquets with such court performances in mind. In the trees to each side we can see the tiny heads of uninvited guests—gardeners perhaps?—who have climbed up to enjoy the performance themselves.

A View of the Amphitheater in the Gardens of Claremount
After Jean La Rocque,
French, 1754

These huge semicircular turf steps were designed by Charles Bridgeman in 1725. Unlike the theaters in the bosquets at Versailles of the previous century, this was not designed for use. In an early Georgian garden, visitors were supposed to use their own imaginations to people the stage.

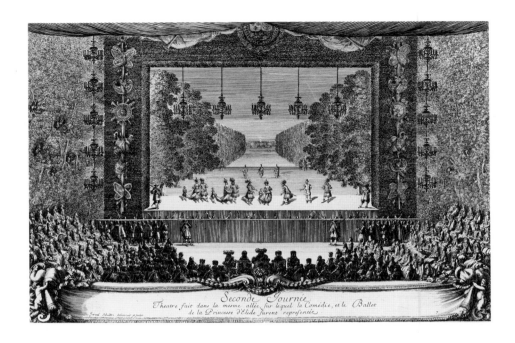

forest to allow horses to follow the hounds more effectively. When French and English gardens expanded into the forests in the 17th century, these patterns in the woods became a standard part of formal garden design.

Elaborate garden fetes with fireworks and pageants had been brought north from Italy along with the gardens themselves. Seventeenth-century Versailles saw the heights of such organized entertainment, but earlier French kings hadn't done badly: Henri III was once greeted at Chenonceaux by bare-breasted court

Tennis Tournament
George Bellows,
American, c. 1921

After the Game
Edwin Howard,
American, 1935

Lawn tennis and badminton supplied the garden theater of the late 19th and early 20th centuries. The flat green used in previous centuries for bowls or dancing became the tennis court. Bellows catches the late afternoon sun pouring over the roof of the Casino at Newport and the easy attitudes of spectators grouped on the lawn and steps. As the dance steps in the print after Vinckeboons must have been familiar to a contemporary viewer, so we recognize what is going on here—one player is about to return a high lob, his partner rushes to the net, while the invisible opponent must be hurrying backwards, hoping to catch the powerful shot.

Architect Edwin Howard, in a sketch from his book *Gazebos and Garden Houses*, shows a natty pair relaxing by a cool lily pond after their game. But while their martinis or manhattans are modern, some garden delights never change. The gazebo could be straight out of a Roman fresco (p. 70), and similar pots of red flowers (these look like petunias) decorated 18th-century French gardens, as in Hubert Robert's *Bathing Pool* (p. 26).

The Blowgun (detail of fan)
French, c. 1765

On a trellised terrace overlooking
a misty Rococo garden, a lady
aims a dart at a bull's-eye
wreathed in flowers. Her compan-
ions, including her little white
dog, look on with admiration, or
perhaps concern, since her
weapon is an Indian blowgun,
certainly capable of inflicting considerable damage on any living
target. Where could she have acquired such a thing? Perhaps from
an explorer or an Indian visitor to
France. In 1725 a group of North
American Indians had been presented to Louis XV. They were
members of a Louisiana tribe that
used similar short blowguns, so
such weapons might not have
been unknown in court circles. We
can imagine that the owner of the
blowgun commissioned this fan as
a permanent record of her exotic
expertise.

ladies disguised as mermaids, who sang before being pursued by satyrs and
rescued by handsome cavaliers. Louis XIV's magnificent fetes of the 1660s,
when he himself was still young and beautiful and an elegant dancer, outdid
them all, however. On one occasion, the youthful Sun King, wearing pink tights
and a headdress of ostrich feathers, performed in a ballet composed for him by
Lully. Artists like Israël Silvestre recorded such scenes in suites of prints.

Over the centuries, artists have noted many of the special spaces carved out
in gardens East and West by the demands of such active pleasures as dancing,
swimming, boating, and, more recently, tennis. Since people like to watch play,
as well as participate in it, there is no wonder that a sense of the garden as
theater pervades many images in this chapter.

A Golden Age

For titillation, fantasy, luxury, and lighthearted gaiety, nothing has ever
surpassed the golden age of garden frivolity in 18th-century France. By the
1760s, the aristocracy had been idling at Versailles for a century. Pleasure and
games of rank passed the time. Artists such as Antoine Watteau, Jean-Honoré
Fragonard, and Hubert Robert captured the long afternoon of the French
aristocracy in all its moods, from poignant nostalgia to steamy sexual promise.
The decorative works of art of the period, including the marvelous fan
illustrated here, have never been surpassed. In fact, elaborate court life was itself
a decorative work of art. In this artificial world the garden, though it too was
artificial, must have seemed a relief from court ritual, and garden games and
fantasies a refreshment.

In 1761 Jean-Jacques Rousseau's revolutionary ideas began to appear in
print, beginning with *La Nouvelle Héloise*, the first romantic novel in the West.

The Swing (detail)
Hubert Robert,
French, late 18th century

At the beginning of the 18th century, a taste arose for *fêtes galantes,* romantic landscapes with tall, mysterious trees and groups of lovers engaged in conversation and amorous dalliance. Hubert Robert celebrates a theme—the girl on a swing—that became symbolic of lovemaking and joyous sexuality. The man pulling the rope raises the woman on the swing to heights of pleasure. The audience includes two gentlemen strategically placed for the best view up the floating skirts of the swinger. Even the huge classical statue of Hercules seems to share in the fun. The painting's sense of exhilaration and unending playfulness typify the spirit of French Rococo garden pleasures.

Garden Scene
Jean-Demosthène Dugourc,
French, early 19th century

During the long centuries before
children were allowed to be children, the garden was a place to let
off steam. The little boy is playing
horsie; his red ribbon reins are
attached to what may be an elaborate horse-powered water pump.
Near the shed a gardener trundles
a wheelbarrow full of watering
cans. There is room for quiet
pleasure in this garden as well; a
man is totally absorbed in his
book, and two ladies in rustic
straw hats gossip in a trellised
bower.

Almost overnight, a passion for passions sprang up, including a passion for nature, especially the kind of nature seen in English landscape gardens. French versions, known as *jardins anglais*, were curvier and more crowded than the English originals. In them, all the aristocracy's aspirations toward Rousseauist freeness and simplicity were enacted in a mad clutter of garden follies and features. English travelers who saw these concoctions made fun of the frenzied French, although, not so long before, the English landscape designer William Kent himself had had his excesses: at one time he recommended planting dead trees in the garden for atmosphere.

About 1750 Cornelis van Loo painted Mme de Pompadour as a pretty gardener in a straw hat. By the 1770s the rage at court for Rousseau and rustic life had reached new heights. Marie-Antoinette spent a million *livres* (roughly the equivalent of $3 million) to make her garden at the Petit Trianon. When she and her best friend, the princesse de Lamballe, sat on a bench together to eat strawberries and cream, everyone wept at their sweet simplicity.

Poetical Pleasures

Less energetic pastimes than tennis, swimming, bowls, and blowguns have always had their place in the garden. The link between wine, poetry, and gardens is celebrated all over the world, but nowhere better than in China. There, a tradition had evolved from Wang Hsi-chih's first literary gathering by a stream, seen in a painting by Ch'ien Ku. To this day, a meandering stream is often built into a Far Eastern garden so that the 4th-century gathering of poets can be reenacted, floating cups and all. In the 18th century an exiled Chinese courtier remembers such a time:

> *Wine-cups floating*
> *while we compete, composing;*
> *you, in laughter, launching a cup for me,*
> *and in my cup, a pearl.*
> (tr. R. Kotewall and N. L. Smith)

Poetry can endow a garden with an aura of allusion and memory. One of the best inscriptions is at Stoneypath in Scotland, the garden of contemporary poet Ian Hamilton Finlay. There, a rather untidy pond is transfigured by four words cut into a lozenge of stone at our feet: "Hear Poussin / See Lorrain." At once we, and the garden, are referred back to—17th-century Rome? 18th-century England? Hanging suspended between the golden landscapes of Claude and Nicolas Poussin's silvery, intellectual history paintings, we see Stoneypath through the prism of all the great gardens inspired by the works of these two artists. Focus again, and we are back at the little pond, which now resonates with meaning.

Mezzetin
Jean-Antoine Watteau,
French, c. 1718

Mezzetin, the amorous and senti-
mental valet character of the
commedia dell'arte, sings of unre-
quited love to an unseen woman,
symbolized by the statue in the
bosquet behind him. The delicious
colors, in a range unusually wide
for Watteau, form a contrast to
the intensity of amorous suffering
we see in Mezzetin's face. Guitar
players will note that the position
of his hands would result in a
sharply defined nasal, almost
twangy, tone.

Love in a Garden

Such flights of imagination brought about by poetry are also part of the story of
love in the garden. Before the invention of romance in the 12th century, Ovid's
Metamorphoses told of the terrible and wonderful loves of the gods. Lovers see
parallels to their stories in the natural metamorphoses of flower and fruit.
Painters and poets alike have used the rose and the medlar tree for symbols of
love and lust. The face of a garden, seen darkly by night, can tell of love ending:

Krishna and Radha: Love in a Bower
Indian, 1780

Sansar Chand, who came to the Kangra throne in 1775, was devoted to the Hindu sacred lovers, Krishna and Radha. To celebrate his marriage at the age of sixteen, he commissioned a series of paintings illustrating Krishna and Radha's love story as told in the *Gita Govinda* (The Song of the Herdsman). The darkness of a flower-spangled bower enfolds the shining pair, while shoots of tender pink and white blossoms spring up on either side of the thicket. Luminous branches overhead, like fireworks descending, enhance the mood of ecstatic sexual union.

Like waking from a fever . . . it is evening.
Fireflies breathe in the gardens on Bellosguardo.
And then the moon steps from the cypresses and
A wave of feeling breaks, phosphorescent—
Moonlight, a wave hushing on a beach.
In the dark, a flame goes out. And then
The afterimage of a flame goes out.
　　from Frederick Seidel, *"Flame"*

Such images of the garden are often used to evoke love, to describe every shade and intensity of feeling, just as gardens have themselves offered lovers the privacy so often missing from their daily lives. Medieval lovers surely preferred the leafy arbor, earwigs and all, to the public great hall of the castle. Japanese lovers like the pair on page 54, who rarely saw each other except in the dark, so many were the curtains, screens, and taboos erected between them, must have welcomed the few moments of light and intimacy they snatched in the garden. Perhaps Krishna and Radha are the most beautiful lovers of all, and the luckiest, freely playing forever in the fragrant groves of Brindaban.

The Pleasures of Fragrance

Whether it is the pungent aroma of box bushes heated by the sun, the faint scent of winter "plum" blossom so beloved in the Far East (actually a species of apricot, *Prunus mume*), or the lilac's opulent cloud of fragrance, perfume fills

Odoratus
French, late 16th century

A golden girl in classical drapery, personifying the sense of smell, sniffs a Madonna lily (*Lilium candidum*) and dandles on her knee an urn filled with lilies, roses, iris, some sort of campanula, a daffodil, and a prized black tulip. She is copied from an engraving of *Odoratus* after Marten de Vos (1532–1603).

View of the Château of Trianon
Jean Rigaud,
French, 1738

It is hard to believe that scent can ever be overpowering in the garden, but the duc de Saint-Simon, the most accurate and amusing chronicler of the court of Louis XIV, says that at the Trianon "the flowers were changed every day, and I have seen the king and court forced to leave because of the tuberoses [*Polianthes tuberosa*], which perfumed the air so strongly that no one could stay in the garden." More than two million pots were used annually in these beds, known as the *parterre fleuriste*.

Garden Fashions

The Flower Garden
Matthew Darly,
British, 1777

Garden pleasures have included
dressing up for a fashionable
saunter around the grounds.
Sometimes, garden fashions come
indoors too. At about the time this
print was made, the duchesse de
Choiseul appeared at court with a
coiffure over 3 feet high, which
displayed a whole garden with a
brook (made of mirror), a jeweled
clockwork windmill, flowers,
and grass.

Petite Robe de Jardin by Poiret
George Barbier,
French, 1913

French couturier Paul Poiret's
elegant dress for the garden contrasts with Darly's grotesque car-
toon. Behind this lady and the bee
headed for her rose stretches a
picturesque garden with a famil-
iar-looking classical temple and
some quite unidentifiable trees.
The grass at her feet is studded
with flowers of exactly the same
shade as her buttons.

the garden air. In the Middle Ages and later, fragrance was valued not just for
the pleasure it gave but because it was thought to ward off sickness, especially
the plague. For George Cavendish, one of Cardinal Wolsey's retainers at
Hampton Court, the scents of the garden had their practical side:

> *My gardens sweet, enclosed with walles strong,*
> > *Embanked with benches to sitt and take my rest*
> > *The knotts so enknotted it cannot be exprest*
> *With arbours and alyes so pleasant and dulce*
> *The pestilent ayers with flavors to repulse.*

The luxury of fragrance is democratic. The gardens of the most ordinary houses in Moorish Granada were filled with myrtle, roses, and the musk rose, famous throughout Islam for its deep perfume. At the other extreme was the garden of Mme de Pompadour at her little Hermitage at Versailles, which was arranged by scent so that one heavenly smell (tuberoses, jasmine, myrtle, and gardenias were her favorites) led to another—blindfolded, she could have found her way among them.

The Garden Gourmet

Gardens have always been places to enjoy picnics, and artists as diverse as Giorgione, Pieter Bruegel the Elder, Manet, Tissot, and Bonnard have painted alfresco meals both plain and fancy. Perhaps the simplest garden picnic, and certainly the earliest, was that apple in the Garden of Eden. The Roman writer Varro (c. 40 B.C.) describes his outdoor dining table set in an aviary—of all places. Later came entrancing fantasies like the stone banqueting table at the Villa Lante at Bagnaia, designed in 1564 by the great Renaissance architect Giacomo Vignola. The river that channels water throughout the garden wells up to cool wine bottles in a trough cut in the table top. The table stands within its own shady enclosure of plane trees: a real garden room with a view of the Roman Campagna.

Other garden picnic spots are more impromptu, and that is part of their charm. Lady Mary Wortley Montagu, dashing and romantic English traveler to the Near East, wrote in 1718 that every evening in their gardens the Turks "choose out a green spot, where the shade is very thick, and there they spread a carpet, on which they sit drinking their coffee, and generally attended by some

slave with a fine voice, or that plays on some instrument." About a hundred and fifty years later, in *Portrait of a Lady*, Henry James described English afternoon tea, another moveable feast:

> *The implements of the little feast had been disposed upon the lawn of an old English country-house in what I should call the perfect middle of a splendid summer afternoon. Part of the afternoon had waned, but much of it was left, and what was left was of the finest and rarest quality. Real dusk would not arrive for many hours; but the flood of summer light had begun to ebb, the air had grown mellow, the shadows were long upon the smooth,*

Overleaf: *The Monet Family in Their Garden*
Edouard Manet,
French, 1874

Manet and Renoir painted this scene side by side and presented their canvases to their host. At one point Manet whispered in jest to Monet, "He has no talent, that boy! Since you're his friend, please tell him to give up painting." Monet gardened in this plot at Argenteuil long before he created his splendid garden at Giverny; it is encouraging to know that he once had such a small and simple place, where the chickens were allowed to stray and a little boy could sprawl on the grass. Pink and white hollyhocks behind the tree echo the colors of Mme Monet's hat and dress. It is impossible to tell accurately what flowers grow in the steeply banked borders circling the lawn but easy to suppose, judging from Monet's stoop and his gentle hand, that he is a practiced gardener who loves what he is doing.

Man Reading in a Garden
Honoré Daumier,
French, c. 1854–1856?

This particularly luminous and transparent watercolor is far removed from the savage restlessness of the political and social caricatures that provided Daumier with a living and made his reputation. A. Hyatt Mayor wrote: "He intended his watercolors—in vain—for people with more sensitivity than the mass public of his lithographs. Accustomed to the intimate scale of a sheet of paper, and set at ease by the cheapness of water paints, he made his watercolors into the most subtle . . . of all his works."

dense turf. . . . The great still oaks and beeches flung down a shade as dense as that of velvet curtains; and the place was furnished, like a room, with cushioned seats, with rich-colored rugs, with the books and papers that lay upon the grass.

Albertus Magnus, Lady Mary's Turkish host, and Henry James are surely an unlikely trio, but all would have agreed that a green lawn dotted with trees is the perfect pleasure ground.

Figure in Hammock, Florida
John Singer Sargent,
American, 1917

The waters of a Florida creek run slowly past the palms of a bungalow garden; a woman is reading, utterly relaxed. Sargent made his only trip to Florida in 1917 to paint John D. Rockefeller's portrait, but a number of watercolors, perhaps the best of his entire oeuvre, were the real accomplishment of his weeks at Ormond Beach. He plunged into the tropical subjects and the intense light of Florida with the abandon of one who has no difficulty indulging himself in such pleasures. His host was Charles Deering, whose industrialist brother, James, was then busy creating the great Italianate gardens of Vizcaya at nearby Brickell Point. Remembering places and gardens in peacetime Europe, Sargent said of Vizcaya: "It combines Venice and Frascati and Aranjuez and all that one is unlikely to see again."

At Ease

By 1874, when Manet painted the Monets in their first simple family garden at Argenteuil, the scale of garden pleasures had changed radically. The great landowners had had their day. As the middle classes grew, and cities and suburbs expanded, the number of small private gardens increased. While everyone continued to enjoy all the immemorial pleasures of the garden, the emphasis changed. The idea of a garden as a retreat, not a rout, became more and more appealing. Artists, particularly the Impressionists and Post-Impressionists, recorded the air, the light, and the passing moment with the same fascination as did Henry James. Instead of painting the gardens of kings or the big private grounds that certainly abounded, they were attracted to the public parks then being developed, and to the pleasures of their own gardens. These were simple countrified plots designed without benefit of Lenôtre or Gertrude Jekyll, but they suited their owners' lives and needs.

The pursuit of happiness in the garden has often been a peaceful affair. Men and women come to refresh themselves in body and spirit. Shade and sun, a place to sit and rest, to read and doze, with perhaps some flowers, are all we ask for, besides fresh air and quiet. Sir Philip Sidney, *preux chevalier* of the Elizabethan Age, sang, "Oh sweet woods, the delight of solitariness! / Oh how well I do like your solitariness!" After the dancing and music, after the flirting and loving, the picnics and the parties, what we finally get to is the heart of it all, the greatest garden pleasure, which is simply being there.

Follies & Features

The amazing "tent" in this Beauvais tapestry would have been recognizable—without the elephant—to any 18th-century European garden aficionado as an elaborate folly. Made of iron, tin, papier-mâché, oilcloth, or canvas and decorated with chinoiserie or Turkish motifs, such tents adorned many a landscape garden. The Chinese *ombrello* at Stourhead, since vanished, was described by a visitor in 1776 as "very pretty, 'tis of painted canvas so remains up the whole year, the inside painted in blue and white mosaic." The best surviving example today is in the royal gardens at Drottningholm in Sweden. The empress of China's little chariot at left would have recalled to any footsore visitor the "chaises bleues" used for transport in French royal gardens. This tapestry is one of nine designs that purport to show the everyday life of the Chinese emperor Kang Xi and may have been inspired by the Jesuit mission to China in 1685.

Exotic tents, sham castles, "ruined" arches, rustic hermitages—all these are garden follies, built to entertain both creator and viewer. One glance at these crazy buildings reveals how they earned their name, for they do indeed seem foolish, if wonderfully so. A folly, though it may serve to organize space as other garden buildings do, is often "separated from ordinary architecture by the eccentricity of its builder," says Barbara Jones, author of *Follies and Grottoes*.

More sober structures, such as garden temples, and useful ones, like bridges, can be called features. While the separation between follies and features is not strict, follies are usually eclectic and fanciful where features generally obey the order and tradition of architecture. Garden statues, too, have tended to follow certain iconographic programs: often they represent classical gods and goddesses or allegorical figures.

In gardens East and West, rock and water are integral to structure and ornament. In the Far East, rocks are valued for their symbolism and individual beauty. In Western gardens, rock has been used in its natural form, since Roman times at least, to make grottoes, artificial caverns that usually house fountains or waterworks. A water feature can be a birdbath, a Rococo cascade, or a stream brimming with iris.

The great age of folly building in Great Britain and Northern Europe was the 18th century. The sky was the limit, but if your own imagination failed you, there was a raft of prints of other people's follies for inspiration. An event described by the redoubtable Mr. Blaikie, who, when it took place, was gardener to the duc d'Orléans at what is now the Parc Monceau, perfectly illustrates the nature of follies and folly builders:

The Marquis de Cray who was allways finding and planning something new, proposed to make buildings of Paper or as he called it Carton. . . . As his highness was always the protector of all new Schemes he let the Marquis proceed in his undertaking, a Most Elegant Dairy for the Suisse Cows. This Miraculous building was framed with thin dales [lathes] upon which they pasted paper and even good white writing paper from Paris. This fabric began with great glee and a great deal of paper allready pasted,

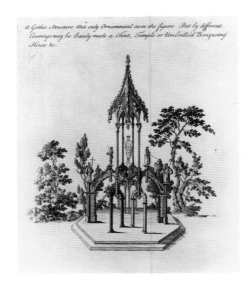

Right: *Party in the Garden of a Castle* (detail)
After David Vinckeboons, Flemish, 1604?

Witch hats of leafy green crown the arbor pavilions, setting the mood for many years of follies to come. Behind the arbor rises a two-story tree house, a feature of many Flemish Renaissance gardens, to judge from the number of garden images in which it appears (see p. 123). To the left is what may be a floral sundial: a circle of low planting surrounds a gnomon formed by a column and a slanted pole. Such sundials first appeared in the 16th century.

Far right: *A Gothick Structure* British, 1759

Who could resist a Gothic building which, according to its caption, was "not only Ornamental" but—with one eye on the English weather—"by different coverings may be Easily made a Tent, Temple or Umbrello'd Banqueting House &c."? The first "gothick" architecture appeared in England in the 1720s. Early gothick follies were delicate and ornate; rustic gothick later became the fashion. Huts and hermitages were built of bark-covered logs. Hermits were hired, but usually didn't last long, as the austere life required by contract—no drink, no girls, no haircuts, and no company—was too much for them.

The Watts Towers
Clarence J. Laughlin, American, 1960

A 20th-century folly was created by Simon Rodia, an immigrant Italian tile-setter working in the Watts section of Los Angeles from 1921 to 1954. He used tile, shells, broken china, and glass set with cement on thin steel to make a huge complex, of which this photograph shows just a tiny detail. Laughlin captures the soaring fantasy that make Watts Towers the rival of any previous folly.

when all of a Sudent a hurrycain of wind and rain happening and all this frail construction was to be found in peaces all over the park and so ended this foolish project.

Of course, many follies were made of such durable materials as flint, brick, and stone, but even some of the more "foolish projects" made of plaster and lathe, almost as frail as the marquis de Cray's *carton*, have survived for over two centuries. Happily for us, many artists delighted in displaying every wild kind of folly in paintings, engravings, and tapestries. It is worth remembering

Perspective View of the Column
French, 1785

The House of the Désert
Belonging to Mr. de Monville
After Constant Bourgeois,
French, 1808

The ultimate folly is, of course, the folly you can really live in. Beginning in 1774, François Racine de Monville spent ten years creating what must be the most strangely magical garden of the 18th century, the Désert de Retz, at the edge of the royal forest of Marly outside Paris. Long abandoned, it is now being restored. There are seventeen follies, ranging from a ruined Gothic church to an icehouse built to resemble an Egyptian pyramid, each situated so as not to conflict with the others, a rare feat indeed in garden design of the period. The star attraction is the ruined column, about 45 feet across and about 60 feet high. Inside are five floors of oval rooms with a central staircase. This plan so enchanted Thomas Jefferson that he adapted it for the Rotunda at the University of Virginia. To the right in the earlier image we can make out the dormers of the kitchen building, connected to the column by a tunnel. Thirty years separate these two views, during which time the trees have grown to fill in and soften the landscape. The artist's sensibility, too, has changed, from the sprightly mood of the Rococo era to the darker, more brooding atmosphere of the Romantic.

that what such images lack is the particular excitement of isolation and surprise real follies possess so abundantly. However, since these fragile buildings are not often restored if they fall or are destroyed, the record in works of art of follies of all kinds, amusing, touching, melancholy, or ridiculous, is a precious roll call of the mad and marvelous in garden history.

Grottoes, Rocks, and Heavenly Caves

Few of us who are not rock gardeners willingly introduce rocks, except for a wall, into the garden today. But for centuries in the West no garden was complete without a grotto. Almost all Italian Renaissance gardens had a rusticated stone grotto from which sprang the water so important to their design and horticulture. But a grotto was more than a simple spring or source; it was also the entrance to the earth, to the underworld. In classical mythology, grottoes had been hiding places for rustic and marine deities. Through the end of the 18th century, garden makers reaffirmed their classical antecedents (and exercised man's eternal curiosity about what lies below) by building grotto homes for nymphs, nereids, tritons, and other watery gods and goddesses. The best grottoes succeeded by virtue of a sort of mineral eclecticism. They were stone pavilions like that at Wilton (p. 33) or fountain surrounds, curiously decorated with shells, flints, hunks of coral, and bits of mirror. Among the most wonderful must have been those designed by the 16th-century French artist and potter Bernard Palissy, whose grottoes were adorned with strangely beautiful ceramic animals glittering in their luster glazes. Equally fantastic were the lacy stalagmites of Salomon de Caus, the engineer, physicist, and landscape architect. A few of the encrusted grottoes of the 18th century, rosy and nacreous

A Roman Grotto
c. 40–30 B.C.

Around the Mediterranean, grottoes have always provided cool, dark relief from the summer heat and blinding sun. The ivy-wreathed entrance here is guarded by a little statue of Hecate, goddess of the underworld, standing to the left of the fountain basin, a hint that someone lives within. Little birds visiting the fountain add their color and song. Above in the sunshine is an airy loggia festooned with vines. The fresco comes from the bedroom of a villa at Boscoreale, which, like Pompeii about a mile to the south, was buried by the eruption of Vesuvius in A.D. 79. The walls of the room were painted to resemble a loggia looking onto a series of different outdoor vistas. This panel is by the window, where the bed was placed.

The Grotto of Narcissus
Salomon de Caus,
French, 1620

De Caus's fountains and grottoes were built all over Northern Europe, where the coolness may not have been as delicious as in southern Italy, but where the magic was just as strong. This one is a pavilion, a common grotto shape; fanciful little trees sprout from the top, perhaps to increase the illusion of being underground. The grotto is made of stone, possibly tufa, a water-pitted, spiky limestone, also known as *pierre antidiluvienne*, much favored by folly builders.

Above right: *A Green Grotto* (detail)
Dutch, c. 1700

This tea cozy of a grotto designed by Jacob Romans, who was architect to William III of Orange and a sculptor at The Hague, is made of trellis and vines. Inside, the grotto is peopled by statues standing in Italian-inspired rockwork, or *rocaille*, niches.

with hundreds of thousands of shells, can still be visited in England, Ireland, and Austria today. Rarely are grottoes satisfactorily depicted in painting or print; we are left with only the rocks, since the real grotto experience of cool darkness, trickling water, and glistening light changes is uncapturable.

Grottoes also stood for the primitive forces of nature, and late 18th-century Picturesque and Romantic versions were correspondingly massy and majestic. Soon the rocks and mountains themselves were perceived as uplifting, and by the middle of the 19th century, people who a hundred years earlier would likely have been making grottoes were building replicas of mountains instead. Later, the rockery or rock garden, with delicate alpine plants and natural-looking rock formations (seldom achieved, alas) gradually but finally took the place of the grotto. The mystery and fantasy had fled, leaving small, dank caverns occupied by plaster saints and gnomes.

In the Far East grottoes symbolized "a passageway through the rocks, through space and time, and the passage was a journey toward enlightenment and happiness, toward renewal and rebirth," as art historian Richard Barnhart points out. The garden represents eternal spring, the paradise we reach through this rocky passage, and the garden grottoes themselves symbolize not only the rocky way to get there, but the heavenly caves of Taoist and Buddhist immortals

*A View of the Great Rock
at Morfontaine*
After Constant Bourgeois,
French, 1808

By the 18th century, huge stones
masqueraded as mountains in gardens. "Take a mountain," said the
sharp-eyed Horace Walpole of
another pile in a similar French
garden, "break it into pieces with
a hammer, number the fragments,
. . . place them in their original
order, . . . plant ivy and grass and
weeds, which will hide the frac-
tures, and so you may have a cart-
load of Snowdon or Penmenmaur
in the middle of your bowling
green."

A Morning Walk
British, 1794

The garden in this fashion plate is
as up-to-date as the ladies' chic
white muslins; 1794 is very early
for the "rock garden" in the foreground, and the palm trees strike
another fashionable note. The
standard rose and the shrubbery
behind are more usual for the
period.

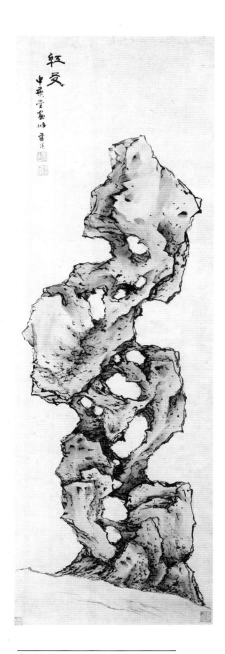

Red Friend
Lan Ying,
Chinese, 17th century

Marvelously eroded Lake Tai rocks have been prized in China since the Tang dynasty (618–906). This hanging scroll shows a favorite, red-tinted rock without its surrounding garden elements, freeing the viewer to imagine its size and context.

as well. Oriental grottoes open into light, where European ones open into eternal darkness and mystery.

Rocks have a resonance and spiritual meaning in Chinese and Japanese gardens that they lack in Europe. Rocks are reminders of sacred mountains, of the holiness of earth and the constant yin-yang energy exchange of Buddhism. It is easy to imagine a Far Eastern garden that is just a solitary rock in an enclosed space. Garden makers and art lovers alike have collected stones of all kinds, and artists of every period have painted them. The best-loved story of "stone lore" may be that of Mi Fei. In 1105, Mi Fei was appointed magistrate in the Wu Wei district, famous for its fine rocks. On his way to pay his respects to his superior for the first time, he entered the official precinct and caught sight of a magnificent rock, perhaps not unlike Lan Ying's *Red Friend*. Forgetting his mission (at least momentarily), he called for his robe and tablet of office and bowed deeply to the stone. It hardly matters what happened to his subsequent career, since Mi Fei lives on forever as the man who truly knew how to behave toward a beautiful garden rock.

Water in the Garden

Moorish gardens in Spain were the first in Europe after the Dark Ages to be filled with sprays of water to cool the air and the senses. It was the Moors who, when Roman engineering knowledge vanished, reintroduced the science of hydraulics in their traditional Islamic gardens, making watercourses, *burladores* (jets), and fountains. Surely the earliest form of air conditioning was that employed by Sultan al-Ma'mun who, in 11th-century Toledo, stayed cool in his magnificent garden by having streams of water poured continuously down the walls of his pavilion.

Fountains and jets are only one kind of water feature. A sophisticated development of the still pool is the water parterre, such as the charming foursquare example at the Villa Lante (dating from the late 16th century), which has a little stone boat in each quadrant, or the grandly curved stone-and-water embroideries laid out by the garden architect Achille Duchêne at Blenheim in the 19th century.

How water is used in gardens of different periods is a sensitive indicator of what society has to say about itself. In the Middle Ages, water filled moats for defense and fish ponds for food. Water in the Renaissance garden, as we have seen, was used with lighthearted formality. At Versailles, long, motionless rectangles extended monarchy and the rules of perspective to the horizon, while impressive fountain statues glorified Louis XIV in the guise of Apollo.

Water has been used to extend the horizon in another way. When the French began to include distant views of the park and countryside as part of the garden, they took down a section of garden wall to do so. To preserve the separation between inside and out, they filled the gap in the wall with a mini-

Spanish Fountain
John Singer Sargent,
American, c. 1914

The color and movement that
water imparts to gardens, especially to the formal courtyards
of Mediterranean countries, are
apparent in this watercolor of an
unidentified fountain in Spain.
Sargent was always fascinated by
the effects of indirect and reflected
light. Here he records three dis-
tinct sources: the warm violet
of the basin reflects light from
below; the putti are highlighted
by sources from the side; and the
rippled surface of the water itself
scatters the sky's reflection.

Winged Infant
Italian, mid-15th century

Only 2 feet tall, this gilt bronze sprite once spouted water, which probably turned a pinwheel device held in his right hand. His feathered ankles suggest an infant Mercury, but that is not borne out by his winged shoulders and a fleecy tail. Attributed to a sculptor who was intimately familiar with the work of Donatello, this putto probably crowned a fountain of the kind Sargent depicted, bringing life and gaiety to the courtyard of some Florentine palace.

moat, called a wet fosse (the English version was the ha-ha, that dry ditch so invaluable to 18th-century landscapers). In English landscape parks, irregular lakes and broad, meandering streams successfully provided calm, shining centers for the whirl of follies, walks, temples, benches, and urns on the surrounding hills and dales.

At West Wycombe in the mid-18th century, the lake was a focus for many of Sir Francis Dashwood's garden high jinks, such as the Turkish tent erected on the island on page 76, the bark under full sail, and the chinoiserie bridge in the distance. Woollett's print exaggerates the size of the baroque rockwork cascade; in fact, it is more modest. Artistic license has also embellished the reputation of Sir Francis and his club, the Monks of Medmenham, whose mild orgies (celebrating black masses in caves under the hill to the right and drinking wine poured by naked girls) have grown immense in legend. The garden itself was reputedly laid out in the form of a naked woman, visible from the steeple of the parish church. In the golden ball on top, barely discernible here, there was just enough room for four Monks to enjoy the view—surely a rather cramped orgy. However, careful search has not yet proved quite how the form of the lady was disposed on the ground, if indeed she ever was.

In all these basins and lakes plants were scarce. With a few exceptions, and those mainly scientific, the kind of water garden filled with water lilies that Monet painted did not become popular in the West until the end of the 19th century. In Japan, water plants have been common in gardens for centuries. Water-loving iris (*I. laevigata*) is usually grown near a *yatsuhashi*, or Eight-Plank Bridge, an association that dates to the 10th century. Even today, the sight of iris blooming near a *yatsuhashi* in a garden will remind all Japanese familiar with their country's literature of the incident from *The Tales of Ise*, a collection of romantic episodes in the life of a courtier. When self-exile from court seemed politic, the hero departed with one or two old friends, looking for a place to settle. They found themselves at a river divided into eight channels, each with a bridge.

Dismounting to sit under a tree near this marshy area, they ate a meal of parched rice. Someone glanced at the clumps of irises that were blooming luxuriantly in the swamp. "Compose a poem on the subject, 'A Traveler's Sentiments,' beginning each line with a syllable from the word 'iris,' " he said. The man recited,

> *I have a beloved wife,*
> *Familiar as the skirt*
> *Of a well-worn robe,*
> *And so this distant journeying*
> *Fills my heart with grief.*

They all wept onto their dried rice until it swelled with the moisture.
(tr. Helen McCullough)

A *View of the Cascade &c. in the Garden of Sir Francis Dashwood, Bart.*
After William Hannan,
British, 1757

Water is the element that holds together this animated landscape, which still exists today in simplified form. In the background is a chinoiserie bridge, adding a touch of the folly to a necessary feature. The village and church of West Wycombe are in the distance on the right. A tent folly is pitched on the small island in the center as a refuge for guests. In the foreground, one sturdy gardener whets his scythe; another continues to mow the vast lawn, while the cut grass is swept up with besoms, or twig brooms.

Each of the five lines of the poem contains one of the five syllables of *kakitsubata*, or iris. The story, like so many Japanese stories, seems slight but is fragrant with suggestion. Love, wit, homesickness, the romance of exile, and the poet's virtuosity, all are packed into just a few words, evoked in their turn by the iris and bridge.

Garden Gods and Goddesses

Besides follies and features, which focus a viewpoint, provide shelter, or inspire melancholy or fun, the presence of sculptures in the garden creates a magical symbiosis of art and landscape that can be as effective with works of the 20th century as it was in the Renaissance. Then, the gods and goddesses of classical antiquity came back in marble and bronze to haunt the groves from which they had once been banished. It was the unearthing of quantities of antique sculpture in and around Rome during the 15th century that triggered the passion for statues. The rediscovery of classical literature, especially Ovid's *Metamorphoses*, provided a ready-made garden iconography. It is fair to say that if Virgil's *Georgics* gave us the model for a garden landscape, Ovid's *Metamorphoses* peopled it. Every god, goddess, and minor deity we know—and some we don't,

Yatsuhashi
Japanese, c. 1800

Album paintings of the great classics of Japan, such as the 10th-century *Tales of Ise*, have a charming freshness and subtlety. Here the high, watery horizon and the *yatsuhashi*, or eight-plank bridge, disappearing into the unknown, make the exiles look as small and lonely as the text describes them. To this day, Japanese gardens have *yatsuhashi* bridges, accompanied by iris, to evoke the tale.

Yatsuhashi
Katsushika Hokusai,
Japanese, c. 1833–1834

By the time Hokusai made this woodblock print of the original Eight-Plank Bridge in the province of Mikawa, it was familiar from repeated use in Japanese gardens. The iris here are reduced to strokes for leaves and scattered dots for flowers. Hokusai has replaced the 10th-century ideal of *yatsuhashi*, usually associated with elegant court nobles and carefully observed iris, with a genre scene in which ordinary people cross the bridge to pursue their daily activities, contemplating the iris as they go.

Mazes and Fences

A Circular Maze
Jan Vredemann de Vries,
Flemish?, 1583

A Hedge Maze at Het Loo (detail)
Dutch, c. 1700

Mazes are of obscure and marvelous origin. The legend of Theseus and the Minotaur makes a good beginning, but we must also add the soldiers' drill, or Game of Troy, described in the *Aeneid*. Turf mazes called Troy Towns still exist in England. Mosaic labyrinths on medieval church porch floors represent miniature penitential pilgrimages; outdoor labyrinths, named *Chemins de Jérusalem*, can still be found near some English churches.

The first garden mazes were meant to divert the eye—low, intricate patterns of herbs and box hedges. When there were few flowers in the garden, scent and evergreen pattern meant much more. In 1563 Thomas Hyall wrote, "Isope and time, or winter savery and time, wyl endure grene al the yeare throw," and recommended their use in mazes.

Hedge mazes, in which to play at getting lost, like the one in William of Orange's great garden at Het Loo, were a comparatively late development. The print also shows other kinds of garden dividers: a sloped, planted bank, trees espaliered against a wall, and, beyond that, an immensely high trellis. Perhaps all this geometry was too much for our artist; performing at the fountain in the middle of this very proper garden is a live *mannikin pis*.

A stout and handsome wattle fence surrounds this late medieval garden, reminder of a time when fences were really needed. Materials traditionally used were osier and willow, tough enough to form a dense, rigid barrier but flexible enough to be woven like a basket. The object is an ivory statuette base, carved as a parody of the temptation of Adam and Eve in the Garden of Eden.

*Common Chinese Fence &
Garden Paling*
British, 1759

Fences can be ornamental as well as useful, framing a garden while protecting it. Design books of the 18th century supplied an endless variety of lattice fences that could be built by any competent estate carpenter. Though the inspiration for many of them was the flood into the West of Chinese paintings and porcelains that showed house railings and balustrades, Europeans quickly began to invent their own chinoiserie patterns. Loath to waste an inch of space, this artist added designs for a teapot, a canister, and tureens.

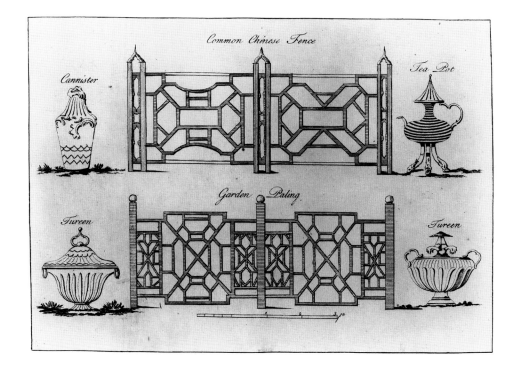

like the mysterious bronze sprite illustrated on p. 75—found a place. We can scarcely imagine the freshness and audacity these creatures must have had for their first dazzled Renaissance viewers, accustomed as we are to the Venus de Milo on a pencil box. New to them after the Middle Ages were these beautiful (mostly) and lifelike images of fertility, license, and sensual pleasure, seen in the half-light of mystery and magic that clings to the idea of metamorphosis.

Many statues placed in gardens were not antique, of course, but contemporary, part of the great outpouring of Renaissance genius. Deities like Flora and Pomona, who were protectors of gardens and orchards, mingled with other gods who had nothing to do with the garden. Some statues, such as those personifying the seasons or representing actual portraits, were not deities at all. At the Villa Pratolino in 1645, John Evelyn enthusiastically noted Michelangelo's "Laundress wringing Water out of a piece of Linnen very naturaly, into a vast Lavor" (this fountain figure, now lost, was actually by Valerio Cioli). Nor were dolphins, deer, and many other animals overlooked. In all, it was a glorious garden party.

Which deities appeared in gardens, and how they were depicted, changed over time. Some garden deities stuck it out in bowdlerized but charming form through the 19th century. Flora, the Italian goddess of flowering plants whose feast was celebrated with indecent farces in ancient Rome, would have been surprised at her later, chaster manifestations.

Other gods disappeared almost entirely. In archaic Greece Priapus had been a powerful fertility god. By Roman times, he had become something of a joke,

Priapus and *Flora*
Pietro and Gian Lorenzo Bernini,
Italian, 1616

When the great Baroque sculptor
Gian Lorenzo Bernini was only
eighteen years old, he joined his
sculptor father in carving these
two large garden statues for Sci-
pione, Cardinal Borghese. Until
the end of the 19th century they
stood at the entrance to the Villa
Borghese in Rome. Their top-
heavy, dwarfish proportions are
not uncommon in statues that
serve as terms, or boundary
guardians. John Evelyn seems to
have admired this charming pair,
since in 1644 he noted that "the
enterance of the Garden, presents
us with a very glorios fabrick, or
rather dore-Case adorned with di-
vers excellent marble statues."

the protector of gardens all right, but more of a scarecrow than a terrifying
presence. When he reappeared in the Renaissance, all that was left of his
original function—and many must have felt it was quite enough—was his
enormous penis, discreetly presented here as a pomegranate poking out of a
basketful of vegetables. The squared-off lower half of his body, and that of his
companion, Flora, are reminders of how often statues were used as architectural
elements. As "terms," images of Terminus, another vanished garden god, they
mark the boundary or terminus of the garden in various ways: at the end of
vistas, or lining the sides of walks or enclosures. Priapus is often shown as a

Two statues and pairs of urns
mark changes of level in this
pleasantly disheveled tapestry
garden. A Hercules in his lion skin
stands on the right, and, with the
figure on the left, perhaps a Bac-
chus, forms a gateway to the flight
of shallow steps. A high trellis
fence divides the staircase from
the level above. Resting after his
clearly not-too-arduous labors, the
gardener's boy sits with a rake
and watering can.

term, perhaps because he is reputed to be the son of Hermes, who as the old
demon god of the wayside was himself often treated as a term or marker. A
common architectural use for statues was as caryatids of stone or wood to
support the roofs of garden buildings or the trelliswork of arbors.

In and around fountains, on terraces silhouetted against the view, two by
two at gates, and at the tops and bottoms of stairs, many of these figures still
stand, monuments to the clear happiness and unbridled, naughty sexuality of

The Triumph of Nature over Art
Pietro da Cortona,
Italian, c. 1633

When Giovanni Battista Ferrari was about to publish his treatise on gardening, *De Florum Cultura*, in 1633, he decided to enliven what he feared might be a dull, practical tome with a few allegorical tales and he commissioned illustrations from Pietro da Cortona. Here a contest takes place between Nature and Art. Art, on her knees with her grafting knife, has produced a rosebush with flowers of three colors. Flora, unimpressed, is about to crown Nature for *her* effort: as if by magic a "Chinese rose tree" (perhaps a variety of rose-mallow, *Hibiscus mutabilis*) has sprung up whose flowers are said to deepen from white to pink to scarlet in the course of a day. Around it in a circle dance Vertumnus, Pomona's lover, holding his *sistrum*, or pan-pipes, and three little boys who represent Dawn, Noon, and Evening.

gardens other than ours. Let us leave them lively, as the Italian writer Sannazzaro saw them in the 1490s:

> But that which pleased me to regard with most attention were certain naked Nymphs, standing half-hidden behind a chestnut bole, laughing at a ram, who, in his eagerness to gnaw a wreath of oak that hung before his eyes, forgot to feed upon the grass around him. At that moment come four Satyrs, with horns upon their heads and goats' feet, stealing through a shrubbery . . . softly, softly, to take the maidens by surprise.

Flora
French, c. 1683

On an embroidered hanging, a
sweet and domesticated Flora,
here also personifying Spring,
looks around from arranging
flowers on a marble plinth. The
tools of her trade, including a
rake, sickle, and a very busi-
nesslike pitchfork, are seen in tro-
phy form below. She is ringed by a
dazzling wreath of flowers of all
seasons, from narcissus to chrysanthemums. The model for Flora
was Françoise-Marie de Bourbon,
Mlle de Blois, legitimized daughter
of Louis XIV and Mme de Montespan. The hanging is one of a set
of eight depicting the Sun King,
Mme de Montespan, and their
children as the Elements and the
Seasons. The designs are attributed to the workshop of Charles
LeBrun, the artist responsible for
the sculpture program in the gardens of Versailles.

Gardens of the Far East

This album leaf by an unknown Southern Sung painter shows a villa garden in the middle distance. The principles of yin and yang give perfect balance to the painting, just as they do to Chinese gardens, by only *suggesting* opposites. The silence of the immense sky brings to mind the imagined sounds of evening—birds, the wind moving the trailing vines in the pine, and quiet conversation in the garden pavilion between the scholar and his young attendant. A tiny full moon rising and the viewer's unspecified vantage point create a sensation of weightlessness, as though one were no longer controlled by gravity, or any other earthly force. Wang Wei, poet, scholar, and garden maker of the 8th century, evokes the same mood in "Birds Calling in the Valley":

Men at rest, cassia flowers falling
Night still, spring hills empty
The moon rises, rousing birds in
the hills
Sometimes they cry in the spring
valley.

No statues of gods or goddesses ornament Far Eastern gardens. Their place is taken by natural objects, especially rocks, or by seasonal spectacles: blossoming plums or cherries, autumn leaves. However, "natural" is always a dangerous word to use about a garden. Alexander Pope's "natural" grotto at Twickenham, studded with flints, chips of mirror, and hunks of quartz, is the least natural rocky cave we can imagine. In the same way, surviving Chinese gardens are crowded and elaborate to Western eyes, and Japanese examples appear mannered in their spare perfection. But like gardens all over the world, those in the Far East have always served the same human needs: they are places for religious and social ceremony, for meditation and repose, for music, laughter, and love.

China, Mother of Gardens

So Ernest Henry "Chinese" Wilson, the great English botanical explorer of the early 20th century, affectionately styled the country where he collected over a thousand species. China's astonishing flora has greatly enriched gardens in temperate climates all over the world. Many of these are plants the Chinese themselves did not cultivate, which grew wild in remote Tibet or western China. Chinese garden philosophy, however, was not transplanted as easily as the peony and the rose. Since the 5th century, Chinese gardens have been retreats not from the wilderness outside, but from the rigid order of daily life.

In China and Japan, man's place in nature is that of a helper, not a ruler. The stability of axial symmetry or the long controlling vista, and the contrast of order within to wilderness without, do not exist in East Asia. A Chinese or Japanese gardener values irregularity, surprise, and the impromptu: showers of leaves or blossoms, trees pruned to asymmetry, and sights that emerge suddenly from behind rocks and walls. When Sen no Rikyū, the 16th-century Japanese tea master, surveyed his garden after the garden boy had swept and tidied, he was dissatisfied. The boy protested that nothing more could be done to make the garden beautiful. Rikyū stepped up to a small maple, brilliant with autumn foliage, and shook it. A few tiny red leaves floated down to the emerald moss below.

Tree Peony and Quince
Ch'en Shun,
Chinese, 1540

Ch'en Shun, one of the greatest
Soochow masters, fills an album
of garden flowers with exuberant
brushwork and great bursts of
sensuous color. Gaiety and
richness are as much a part of
Chinese gardens as austere rocks
and pines. Here the artist depicts
earliest summer with fiery Japanese quince (*Chaenomeles japonica*) and the tree peony's soft
colors and tender outlines. The
tree peony (*Paeonia suffruticosa
syn. moutan*) has been prized in
China since the 3rd century A.D.
The intense pleasure of watching
time unfold in the sequence of
garden flowers is a favorite theme
of Chinese artists. Five centuries
before this joyous painting was
made, the poet Ou-Yang Hsiu
expressed the same happy
hedonism, with some advice on
garden design:

> The light and the deep, the red
>   and the white should be
>   spaced apart;
> The early and the late should
>   likewise be planted in due order.
> My desire is, throughout the
>   four seasons, to bring wine along,
> And to let not a single day pass
>   without some flower opening.

Recognizing change as the only constant aspect of existence, makers of East
Asian gardens never strive for the impossible: permanence. Instead, transience
and the continual shifting balance between the yin-yang opposites of light and
dark, stillness and movement, shape and void are given tangible form in the
garden. The process of making a garden is considered an essential part of yin-
yang balance. By planting a tree, or playing water against rock, the garden
maker becomes part of the universal exchange of energy. Walking through the
garden, ideally we too participate in that process of transformation. A single
rock, for instance, becomes a mountain in the imagination. The airy, empty
spaces in Southern Sung paintings (1150–1250) allow for the same creative
exchange with the viewer. We sense a similar involvement with process in the
works of such painters of gardens as Ch'en Shun (1483–1544), who reveled in
patterns of color and ink, enjoying the brush line with comparative indifference
to actual representation.

What kinds of gardens were recorded in Chinese works of art? Over the
centuries, three very different kinds of garden evolved: the scholar's garden for
study, contemplation, and entertainment; imperial gardens for display and for
the pleasures of the court; and temple gardens for ritual and prayer as well as
contemplation and study. Unfortunately, temple gardens have literally vanished;
there are few representations in art, and almost no temple precincts survive
today.

The Scholar's Garden

The idea for the scholar's garden sprang out of hermits' residences of the Han
dynasty (206 B.C.–A.D. 220). These were the simple retreats of virtuous men
who had left the world for contemplation, peace, and study. One such, the
hermit Yen Kuang, built a little fishing platform by the river. Another, the herb
gardener Han K'ang, disappeared into the mountains. Most quixotic of them all
was surely the scholar Tung Chung-shu, so preoccupied by his thoughts that for
three years he did not even glance out at his garden! For many centuries
following, certain garden features commemorated these men—a hut by a pond
stocked with fish, a patch of herbs, a study-library overlooking a view. Even
such fragmentary suggestions as the herbs or the hut were considered sufficient
to evoke these historical personalities. Chinese scholars' gardens remained
simple. As Richard Barnhart has written: "A clump of bamboo by a courtyard
wall or a small pavilion suitably sited was all that was necessary. A wall
enclosing space defined a private precinct, and that precinct would be
understood to be apart—to be a garden."

View of a Garden Villa (details)
Yüan Chiang,
Chinese, c. 1700

A lawn is unheard of in a Chinese
garden. The surface in the foreground of this handscroll detail is
probably covered with round pebbles. The gentlemen and their
attendants stand on unglazed ter-
racotta tile, while to the left the
ground is most likely covered with
sand or fine gravel. The itinerary

Palace Gardens

An imperial garden, or a garden belonging to a great family, was larger, more
elaborate, and more open—a completely realized landscape one could walk
through and live in. In a rare portrait of such a garden, the Gazing Garden in
Nanking, we see every conceivable kind of pavilion and enclosure, path, pond,
rock, grove, and wall.

Imperial gardens of China and 12th-century Japanese "boating-style"
gardens of the Heian court, like those described in *The Tale of Genji*, were the
playgrounds of brilliant aristocratic societies living in enforced idleness. But the

of this garden in Nanking, the Chan-yüan, or Gazing Garden, must have been very like that of the garden in *The Dream of the Red Chamber*, the great 18th-century Chinese novel of manners. In the book a party of Chinese nobles strolls around the circuit walk, naming each pavilion and rock, capping each other's couplets and literary allusions. This itinerary of garden "incidents," which included a crooked cave, a square pavilion, and a round belvedere, reads much like that of an 18th-century European landscape garden, although a glance at any engraving of one will illustrate the vast difference in practice. But what the Chinese strollers share with landscape-garden enthusiasts such as Alexander Pope and Thomas Jefferson is the sense that a garden is only half a garden without inscriptions to summon and focus the viewer's feelings. In another detail of the Chan-yüan handscroll, a rustic *ting*, or pavilion, is perched atop a "mountain" built of rocks piled on top of one another. Chinese gardens were a revelation to Europeans because of their naturalistic asymmetry, but they are nonetheless creations of clever artifice. Innumerable yin-yang associations are activated by the garden "mountain"; the massive rocks are punctuated with eroded voids, while the dark, enclosing grottoes contrast with the bright surface of the white wall.

purpose of these gardens, despite their size and splendor, was not very different from that of the scholar's garden. The emperor Ch'ien-lung (1711–1799) wrote:

> *Every emperor or ruler must, upon retiring from his official duties and audiences, have a garden in which to stroll, to look around and have rest for his heart. If he has a suitable place for this, it has a refreshing effect upon his mind and regulates his feelings, but if not, he becomes engrossed in sensual pleasures and loses his strength of will.*

In both China and Japan, such large pleasure gardens had religious significance as well. They represented the Western Paradise—the Buddhist Pure Land—a heaven envisioned by the followers of the Amida Buddha, who believed that by the simple recitation of the Buddha's name they would reach such a garden nirvana. By the 3rd century A.D. the first Chinese translations of sutras about the Pure Land were available. These Buddhist teachings described parks, palaces, and gardens filled with lotus lakes of perfumed water, fragrant flowers, and trees of coral and gold. In Japan, from the time Buddhism was introduced in the 6th century, Pure Land lay believers existed side by side with monks who sought salvation through rigorous self-enlightenment. In both China and Japan, monks used their gardens as aids to meditation, while Amida Buddhists strolled and boated through their paradises.

Making the Garden

The first step in making a Chinese garden is to excavate for water, not just because water is necessary for the life of plants, but also because it provides the fundamental contrast of opposites: the fluidity and movement of water and the immovability of stone. Then the space is defined: walls, used from the 13th century on for surrounding important precincts, are constructed to create an enclosure and to divide the interior space into surprising, irregular courtyards. As the final step, contrasting elements such as rocks and plants that illustrate the principles of yin and yang are introduced, and the life of the garden begins. Only a limited range of plants was used in gardens or seen in garden paintings. A wider variety is seen in paintings of individual flowers. Trees and shrubs most commonly planted include mulberry, catalpa, willow, and the "three friends of winter": pine, bamboo, and plum. Because these last three are steadfast, meaning their essential characteristics of tenacity, flexibility, and rejuvenation recur annually, they were singled out as "virtuous plants" corresponding to Confucian ideals. Quite naturally, too, because of their beauty at all seasons of the year and their hardiness, gardeners have always been eager to use them.

Mei hua, the flowering plum tree (*Prunus mume*), known as the third "friend of winter," is enveloped in a cloud of paintings, poems, meanings, and memories. Of all flowers, it is the one most intimately associated with the

Lotuses on a Summer Evening
Yün Shou-p'ing,
Chinese, 1684

This hanging scroll is by one of
the few Chinese flower painters to
attain the stature of the great
landscape artists. The lotus
(*Nelumbo nucifera*) is the symbol
of purity and a passage to a higher
life, since its peerless flowers rise
from the muddy depths into air
and light. Amida Buddha is traditionally shown enthroned on one
of its beautiful glaucous leaves. In
fact, the famous lotus-filled lakes
of the Summer Palace in Peking
look more like fields of cabbage
than the shimmering vegetal lakes
of legend. Perhaps the sensuous
experience of a Chinese water
garden is better conveyed by Yün
Shou-p'ing's masterpiece and by
the poem he inscribed upon it:

> *Suspended shadows, thin stalks*
> *toy with clouds and rippling*
> *water,*
> *A scented breeze seems to rise*
> *off the Ink Pond.*
> *Dew wets red garments, golden*
> *powder falls,*
> *Like dusky fragrance, a worn*
> *body receives their cool wind.*
> (tr. Richard Barnhart)

The Three Friends of Winter
Chinese, c. 1150–1250

This detail of a Southern Sung handscroll is the oldest representation in the Metropolitan Museum of the "three friends." At left is the pine, patriarch of trees and a symbol of virtue for everyone from Confucius to Mao Tse-tung. Pines create the impression of age, like garden rocks; a pine tree depicted with a crane stands for longevity. The lush bamboo is valued for its color, movement, the wonderful sound made by its leaves, and its simplicity and integrity of shape. Su Shih, the Sung poet, said, "Without meals one becomes thin; Without bamboo one becomes vulgar." The plum by the fence at right is perhaps the most commonly depicted tree in Far Eastern art.

Chinese in art, literature, and everyday life. The fragile, short-lived blossoms and the rugged, long-lived tree have given rise to two contrasting personae: the "plum blossom beauty," pale, spiritual, and elegantly unadorned, and the "flowering plum recluse," who endures in virtue and solitude. In a couplet as slight and beautiful as a young plum tree itself, the 10th-century poet Lin Pu, the first of those known as flowering plum recluses, captured the asymmetrical look of the tree, its much-prized subtle fragrance, its ideal placement in a garden, and the perfect time to view the blossoms—by moonlight:

> *Its sparse shadows are horizontal and slanted—the water is clear and*
> *   shallow.*
> *Its hidden fragrance wafts and moves—the moon is hazy and dim.*
>   (tr. Hans Frankel)

Devotion to the flowering plum reached absurd heights by the middle of the 12th century. One intoxicated poet munched the very blossoms as a midnight snack, claiming: "Fresh verses issue from my mouth; fragrant in every word." The most obsessive plum devotee was certainly Chang Tzu, who filled a 10-acre garden with hundreds of flowering plums and wrote a sublime and silly guide for plum-blossom cultists. For example, the blossoms should remain "unstained by smoke and dust" and be properly glorified by "subtle artists with plain ornaments and makeup [plum blossom beauties] singing elegant songs." But watch out, says Chang, the blossoms will be mortified if they are "planted under the window of a vulgar monk," or if "dog droppings are found under the tree."

Chinese gardens grew more elaborate over time until by the late 19th century they bore an uncanny stylistic resemblance to Victorian gardens in their multiple features and muddled but charming layouts. What remained unchanged throughout the long history of Chinese gardens, however, was the ideal of a garden as a place to meditate, to find release, to celebrate the passing seasons, and to store memories.

The Pure Whiteness of Winter
Hsü Ching,
Chinese, 1441

Nine hundred years before this
hanging scroll was painted, the poet
Hsiao Kang first captured the soul
of plum, transforming a tree in a
palace garden into that ideal woman,
the "plum-blossom beauty."

> *In the many-walled palace's*
> *Sacred garden:*
> *Marvellous trees, a myriad kinds,*
> *And smaller plants in*
> *thousandfold profusion,*
> *With lights diffused and*
> *shadows mingled,*
> *Twigs abound and trunks are*
> *everywhere. . . .*
> *The flowering plum is the*
> *earliest to blossom,*
> *She alone has the gift of*
> *recognizing spring.*
> *Now, receiving yang, she brings*
> *forth gold,*
> *Now, mingling with snow, she*
> *wears a cloak of silver.*
> *She exhales glamor and lights*
> *up the grove all around her,*
> *She spreads splendor at the*
> *meeting of five roads.*
> *As jades are joined and pearls*
> *strewn,*
> *So ice is hung and hail spread.*
> *Tender leaves sprout, not yet*
> *formed;*
> *Branches pull out fresh shoots*
> *and stick them onto old twigs,*
> *Petals from the treetop fall*
> *halfway and fly in the air,*
> *Sweet scent goes with the wind*
> *to faraway places.*
> *She suspends slow-drifting*
> *gossamer*
> *And mingles with heavy*
> *morning mist.*
> *She competes with cosmetic*
> *powder dropped from upstairs*
> *And surpasses silk on the loom*
> *in sheer whiteness.*
> *Now, breaking into flower, she*
> *leans on a hillside,*
> *Now, reflecting her own image,*
> *she overhangs a pond.*
> *Stretching towards jade steps,*
> *she forms brilliant patterns;*
> *Gently brushing a carved door,*
> *she lowers her branches.*
> (tr. Hans Frankel)

Planting Chrysanthemums
Lu Chih,
Chinese, c. 1550

This delicately painted scene from a hanging scroll brings to mind some of the deep pleasures of working in the garden: the smells of dirt and fresh autumn air, the rhythms of digging and planting, the beauty of the plants, the delight of sharing the garden with friends when the work is done. Lu made the scroll for his friend Tao, visible outside the gate to the right, who has come with a gift of chrysanthemum seedlings. On the veranda, the artist portrays himself showing a helper where to plant more chrysanthemums along the fence of his modest hermitage garden.

Japanese Gardens

In Japan, the same three types of gardens developed as in China—scholars', palace, and temple gardens. The Japanese also created the austere sand-and-rock temple gardens and the tea gardens inspired by Zen Buddhism. A strong Chinese influence on gardens has prevailed continuously in Japan since the 7th century A.D., when Buddhism was introduced from China via Korea. But Japanese gardens are not mere copies of the Chinese. Just as the palace gardens

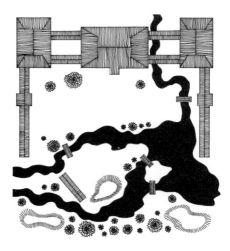

Heian Mansion and Garden

The central building of the classic Heian mansion faced south and was flanked on east and west by outbuildings. Corridors were pushed out in front of the outbuildings to join each to a pavilion, so that the main group of buildings and corridors formed a south-facing rectangle. The court and the open space beyond were used for the principal garden, consisting of a lake, a pine island, a stream, one or two artificial hills, grasses, flowering plants, and white sand. The feeling of this garden, seen from within the main room of the house, the *moya*, or mother chamber, was of intimacy and closeness to nature.

at Schönbrunn or Caserta are characteristically Austrian or Neapolitan, though they are modeled after Versailles, so gardens in Japan are distinctive in their spatial arrangements, plantings, and meanings.

What gave these gardens their special character from the very beginning? Chinese gardens had been Buddhist-inspired since the first century A.D., while in Japan Shinto beliefs based on the worship of natural phenomena shaped the earliest concepts of landscape. Objects such as trees and rocks were singled out and worshiped for their size, shape, age, or beauty. The immanent spirits of places—mountains, springs, and waterfalls—were also venerated. Such sacred areas were marked off with ropes or stones. Perhaps the first of the many Japanese words for garden (still in use today) was *niwa*, which means "pure place." Since worshipers must be cleansed before entering, water is always present. Paths are the final necessary element in a Japanese garden composed of water, rocks, and trees.

In places where a variety of spirits are worshiped, people make their way along paths connecting the various roped-off sacred groups. Often these paths are spread with gravel or small stones; the crunch beneath the worshiper's feet helps him reach a calmer state of mind, removed from daily life. The 5th-century shrine of the Sun Goddess at Ise, which still exists today, is a simple wooden building with a bark roof set in an ancient natural forest near a small river. This type of nearly unshaped, parklike landscape was the foundation on which later Chinese-inspired gardens were built.

The Ugly Artisan

The building of the earliest "Chinese" garden in Japan is described in a 7th-century text known as the *Nihongi*. The story goes that one day a man from Korea named Michikō arrived in Japan. Because he was ugly, the Japanese planned to banish him to a distant island, but Michikō let it drop that he knew how to build "mountain shapes." Not long before his arrival, word had reached Japan of the stupendous garden built by the Chinese emperor Yang Ti (A.D. 589–617). Called the Western Park, it was sixty miles around and filled with lakes, hills, pavilions, and rocky islands. Could Michikō make such a garden, with its much-prized island rock forms, for the Japanese empress? Of course. All talk of banishment ceased. He was renamed the "Ugly Artisan" and set to work at the imperial palace; the race to have the most fashionable Chinese-style island garden was on. In early Japanese gardens, these rocky islands *were* the garden—for many centuries the word *shima* or *jima*, meaning island, also meant garden. At the Mii-dera temple near Ōtsu, a group of three stones erected in A.D. 670 stands at the edge of what once was a lake. Perhaps directly inspired by the work of the Ugly Artisan, they are arranged in the traditional "Heaven, Earth, Man" formation still used in Japanese flower arrangements today.

Gardens of The Tale of Genji

Many of the pictures in this chapter show fragments of gardens rather than the panoramic views so familiar in Western art. Perhaps this artistic convention sprang partly from the design concept of the large, classic Japanese garden, which is never visible all at once but is instead "unrolled," not unlike a scroll painting, by the contemplative viewer strolling around the garden paths or boating around the lake shore.

By the end of the 9th century, the first wave of Chinese taste in garden design had been assimilated, and gardens were built reflecting Japanese as well as Chinese landscapes. By that time outdoor entertainments had already taken their preeminent place in Japanese life. So there was space in these large Heian gardens for active sports like riding, archery, and a kind of soccer, for quieter pursuits such as music and dance competitions, fishing expeditions, and boat rides on the extensive lakes, and for celebrations of the passing seasons.

The incomparable *Tale of Genji*, the acknowledged masterwork of Japanese literature, shows us these boating-style gardens with all their pleasures. A 10th-century novel written by Lady Murasaki, lady-in-waiting at the imperial court, *The Tale of Genji* sums up Japanese culture and the strength of its garden aesthetic, not just for its own time but for long after. The novel has been illustrated by countless artists; their illustrations, as well as the descriptions in the book itself, have had an impact on real gardens. In the great 17th-century garden of Katsura, created 700 years after *The Tale of Genji* was written, many of the views were intended to recall scenes from the book.

The story of Genji, son of an emperor by the favorite concubine, recounts his romances with countless women of every class and every kind of personality and looks. Most of these women are not characterized directly but are revealed in their psychological complexity through the descriptions of their gardens. Genji builds a new palace to house his collection of women, giving each of his four favorites her own quarters and garden. Inevitably, as there are four women, there are four gardens, one for each season.

Spring and autumn in the Far East are the most important seasons because they pass so quickly; they are the precious symbols of transience. The spring garden belongs to Murasaki, the author's namesake. Spring is especially appropriate for this beautiful child-woman whom Genji has raised himself, shaping her to be his ideal, just as he has shaped her garden.

> *To the southeast he raised the level of the ground and on this bank planted a profusion of early flowering trees. At the foot of this slope the lake curved with special beauty, and in the foreground just beneath the windows, he planted borders of cinquefoil, red-plum, cherry, winteris, kerria, rock-azalea and other such plants as are at their best in the springtime; for he knew that Murasaki was an especial lover of the spring.*
> (tr. Arthur Waley)

Autumn Wreaths
Japanese, 19th century

Motifs from *The Tale of Genji* were often used to decorate "literary" objects; this lid of a lacquer writing box is an example. The naturalism of its circlets of hemlock, Mugo pine, nandina, chrysanthemum, and other plants makes us think of Akikonomu's gift to Murasaki of autumn leaves and flowers arranged on an ornamental box.

Above right: *A Sprig of Pine*
Japanese, 19th century

On the veranda overlooking this garden lies a pine sprig reminiscent of Murasaki's return gift to Akikonomu. Compressed to fit the side of a tiny lacquer incense box, the scene, with plum tree, pine, rocks, and a stream, instantly conveys the classic Japanese garden inside its cozy *takegaki*, or thatched bamboo fence.

After Murasaki, the most important lady is Akikonomu, described as "small and delicately moulded . . . quiet and very much in control of herself." The somber beauty of an autumn garden of foliage perfectly suits her reserve.

Akikonomu's garden was full of such trees as in autumn-time turn to the deepest hue. The stream above the waterfall was cleared out and deepened to a considerable distance; and that the noise of the cascade might carry further, he set great boulders in mid-stream, against which the current crashed and broke. It so happened that, the season being far advanced, it was this part of the garden which was now seen at its best; here, indeed, was such beauty as far eclipsed the autumn splendour even of the forests near Oi, so famous for their autumn tints.
(tr. Arthur Waley)

Just as comparison of the seasons is a constant theme in Japanese art and literature, so friendly competition exists between the women. They vie for Genji's attention, and they also compete to show who can display the most exquisite taste by exchanging gifts of flowers from their gardens with poems attached. One day in autumn Akikonomu arranges leaves and flowers on the lid of an ornamental box—a gift recalled by this lid of a lacquer writing box wreathed with plants. Her poem is the gentlest challenge: "Your garden quietly awaits the spring./ Permit the winds to bring a touch of autumn." Over the

The Giant Snowball
Attributed to Tosa Mitsutada,
Japanese, c. 1750

The moon turned the deepest
recesses of the garden a gleam-
ing white. The flower beds were
wasted, the brook seemed to
send up a strangled cry, and the
lake was frozen and somehow
terrible. Into this austere scene
he sent little maidservants, tell-
ing them that they must make
snowmen. Their dress was
bright and their hair shone in
the moonlight. Rather outdoing
themselves, several of them
found that they had a snowball
which they could not budge.
Some of their fellows jeered at
them from the east veranda.
　Lady Murasaki, *The Tale*
of Genji
　(tr. Edward Seidensticker)
Between Genji and Murasaki and
the girls in the snow lies the *en*—
the veranda that links garden and
house. *En* is a Buddhist term
meaning "relationship"; it typifies
the interweaving of indoor and
outdoor spaces so integral to Japanese life.

bridges and through the galleries of the palace the box goes to Murasaki, who is
caught short with not much in her garden to send back. Quickly she makes an
arrangement of pine, moss, and stones, with the message "Fleeting, your leaves
that scatter in the wind./ The pine at the cliffs is forever green with the spring."
Genji reproves the clever Murasaki: "I think you were unnecessarily tart—you
should wait until your spring trees are in bloom."

　The garden descriptions in *The Tale of Genji* are more than character
delineation. They are used to express the subtlest shifts of mood. When Genji
learns that Murasaki feels slighted by his attentions to another woman, he visits
her to make peace and spends the whole day in her rooms. Murasaki's icy, silent
unhappiness and Genji's rather desperate efforts to right things are captured in a
brief description of Murasaki's snowy garden seen by moonlight. These same
delicate shades of feeling are also experienced in real Japanese gardens; evoking
them, in fact, is fundamental to Japanese garden design.

Bamboo and Plum
Japanese, 17th century

Young bamboo shoots push up through the snow, and the plum tree bursts into flower. A thousand years of gardening lie between this Momoyama screen and the Southern Sung painting of the "three friends of winter" seen on page 91. After the end of the 17th century, there were few important new developments in Japanese gardens, which increasingly were filled with literary and scenic allusions, as garden design grew much more rigid.

The Garden Grammar

Because *The Tale of Genji* is the classic work of Japanese fiction, and because repetition and imitation are important in garden design as in every other Japanese art form, gardens exist in modern Japan with which Genji would be instantly familiar. It is not just that 11th-century gardens have been preserved— some that old do still exist—but that the meanings and moods of Japanese gardens throughout history exhibit an unparalleled continuity. Each season and time of day has its own customs—viewing the cherry-blossom, for instance, the snow, or the moon—and each is interpreted slightly differently by new generations. The same shapes and groupings of rocks and the same association of certain trees with one another (plum, bamboo, and pine, for example) recur with amazing frequency, constituting the very grammar of the garden, both in reality and in art.

The first enunciation of the art of gardening in Japan was a remarkable book, the *Sakuteiki*, or *Memoranda of Garden Making*, written by a Fujiwara prince, Yoshitsone, toward the end of the 12th century. Much space is devoted to rock islands and waterfalls, less to plants, which were never as important as water, rocks, and hills. The *Sakuteiki* codifies many garden traditions that were supposed to bring good luck. One such was the belief that the Japanese garden stream should run from east to west, following the sun. A seasonal sequence

of trees often follows the same directional path: "Flowering trees should be
planted on the east [for spring] and red maples on the west [for autumn]." The
Sakuteiki is timeless, containing the kind of advice to be found in any Western
garden handbook today. Read, for example, this note about plants for a
streambed: "Don't put those which will grow too fast or too large, but rather
use small wildflowers like balloon flower [*Platycoden grandiflorum*] and hosta
lilies [*Hosta coerules*]."

Zen Rocks and Tea Gardens

Why, in the 14th century, did the Japanese cease to build elaborate palace
gardens filled with flowering trees? Zen Buddhism spread from China
throughout Japan in the Muromachi period (1392–1568), and with it traveled
the aesthetic of Sung-inspired ink landscapes—bare suggestions of mountain,
tree, and stream. The abstraction of image these landscape paintings represent
was what led to the creation of Zen rock gardens.

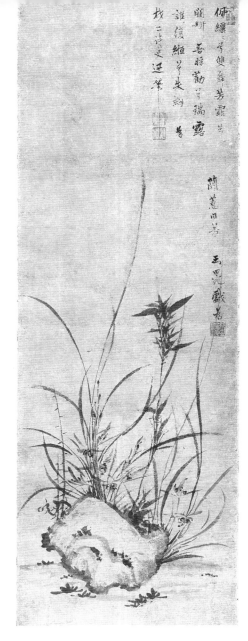

Orchids and Rock
Gyokuen Bompo,
Japanese, late 14th–early 15th
century

The orchid's faint smell is symbolic of the scholar's virtue. Such a scroll as this would originally have been hung in a temple at a gathering of literati priests. Years later it might have found a home in the alcove of a tearoom. The grace and reticence of this ink-on-paper painting can be seen in tea gardens today.

The Zen belief that the universality of Buddha is present in even the simplest stone meant that gardens were pared to their essentials. Flowers were moved indoors to be used almost exclusively in arrangements, and flowering trees were kept in their own part of the landscape or admired on the wild hillside. Zen gardens were designed to reveal eternal, unchanging beauty through the sparing use of evergreen shrubs, trees, rocks, and sand.

Kare sansui (dry landscape) gardens reached their apogee around 1490 in the monastery garden at Ryōanji, a rectangle of sand studded with five mysterious groups of rocks, the most abstract and mystical garden in the world. About twenty years later, a *kare sansui* garden was created at the Daisen-in, another Kyoto monastery. The design of this garden has been attributed to Sōami, painter of the screen illustrated here. He painted a set of twenty sliding doors for the Daisen-in and laid out a number of other gardens. Just as George Washington slept in every American bed, Sōami has been erroneously credited with most of the great *kare sansui* gardens of the period, but the Daisen-in attribution is probably accurate.

The tea ceremony, another Zen practice, has had a profound influence on garden design. The tea garden, or *roji*, meaning "dewy path," leads the participants to the simple tea house, as it prepares their spirits and imaginations for the tea ceremony. Legend has it that tea leaves sprang from the eyelids of the Zen patriarch, Boddhidharma. Because he continually fell asleep when he wished to meditate, he cut his eyelids off and threw them to the ground. Up sprang shrubs with dark, glossy leaves and little fragrant flowers like camellias (*Thea sinensis*, or tea, is a member of the camellia family); the drink brewed from these leaves causes wakefulness. More practically, Japanese gardens owe much to the tea masters who ordained that in the *roji* there should be a stone basin for ritual washing, a stone lantern to see the basin by at night, and a set of stepping stones that lead to the door. Before the rage for tea arose in the 16th century, none of these had been seen in Japanese gardens.

The simplicity of spirit in the tea garden, the last important development in the Japanese garden, leads straight back to the Taoist scholar-recluses in China who had fled to the mountains to save their souls. Sen no Rikyū, the tea master who shook red leaves onto green moss earlier in this chapter, insisted that simplicity was the heart of the ceremony. He repeats the longing for a sylvan, as well as spiritual, retreat in this poem:

> *In the distance*
> *Neither flowers nor maple leaves*
> *Are to be seen;*
> *Only a thatched hut beside the bay*
> *In autumn's twilight.*

The history of Oriental gardens is the history of an art—an art practiced fitfully in the West. Only in Renaissance Italy, in 17th-century France, and in

Landscape of Four Seasons:
Spring
Attributed to Sōami,
Japanese, early 16th century

The serenity and concentration
expressed in Sōami's screen painting reflect the spirit of a Zen
garden. In the painting, clouds of
mist rising from rain-soaked
mountains are enough to indicate
the coming of spring. In a real
garden, rocks, sand, and a few
evergreens offer a similarly spare
sketch of an imaginary world into
which the viewer's mind is drawn.
During the first decades of the
16th century, the great Zen temples of Japan were imbued with
a deep appreciation of Chinese
scholarship and aesthetics. Sōami,
like many other artists of his time,
worked in the Chinese manner, in
muted tones of ink on plain paper.

18th-century England were gardens made and looked upon as serious works of
art; some are even considered supreme works of art of their time. In China and
Japan, however, gardens have always ranked with painting, sculpture, poetry,
and the great romances as expressions of human genius. (The Ryōanji may be
the only "signed" garden in the world: its two creators left their signatures on
the back of one of the rocks.)

It was not, however, with the garden art of the Far East that Marco Polo,
Matteo Ripa, and other explorers returned to Europe. Instead they brought with
them a grab bag of exotic architectural elements, half-understood ideas about
garden design, many new plants that more than anything else altered the
European landscape, and a rich farrago of dragons and houris. Europeans
learned to cultivate the flowers expertly, and out of tales of Xanadu and
Cambulac they concocted some of the world's most ravishing gardens, both real
and imaginary.

A Tray Garden (detail)
Japanese, 14th century

This hanging scroll depicts an arhat being waited on by a little grotesque bearing a rock in a dish—the oldest representation of a *bon-kai* in the Metropolitan Museum. Landscapes in miniature, *bon-kai* (tray gardening) and *bon-sai* (the dwarfing of trees), are a garden art native to the Far East. In addition to plantings, such landscapes often contain pools of water and mountains made of exquisite small rocks. The garden, already reduced to a few elements, is now reduced in its proportions as well. Concentrated attention and a leap of the imagination are required to appreciate it.

Opposite: *A Bon-sai Garden*
Yüan Chiang, Chinese, c. 1700

A detail from the Chan Yüan handscroll shows that this Nanking garden, like most Chinese and Japanese gardens, had an area set aside for *p'en ching*, which became *bon-sai* in Japan. Carefully tended, *bon-sai* can live for many centuries. Since dish landscapes dry out quickly and are susceptible to wind damage, they need a sheltered spot outdoors. Here they can be enjoyed as a group from inside the house as well.

103 GARDENS OF THE FAR EAST

CHAPTER SIX

Botanical Treasure

The Concert
British, c. 1706

When this wool and silk tapestry was woven at John Vanderbank's Soho factory, hardly any distinctions were being drawn between the countries of the Far East. All were part of that marvelous imaginary land, Cathay. These floating islands are peopled with glittering Chinese and Indian figures, the latter based on Mughal miniatures brought back to England in the late 17th century. The horsemen and their attendants are Turkish. The plants are rendered with great detail and enthusiasm but little accuracy; scarcely one can be properly identified. However, real exotic plants were beginning to reach Europe in numbers by this time, and a few, mostly trees and shrubs from North America, soon appeared in gardens.

About 225 species of plants were commonly grown in European gardens during the Middle Ages. Today a typical sales catalogue lists over 1,800 ornamental plants, most of which can be grown in Europe as well as in America. Plant hunters who have enthusiastically brought back exotic trophies from all parts of the globe during the last 250 years are primarily responsible for this increase. The work of hybridizers has done the rest. But plant hunters have been around for much longer than 250 years. Perhaps the first we know about is a woman— Queen Hatshepsut of ancient Egypt—who organized a plant-hunting expedition to Ethiopia more than 3,000 years ago. Several plants brought back from this trip are pictured on the walls of her temple at Luxor.

The discovery of new species and their introduction into the European landscape occurred in many different ways. The importation of some plants was utterly inadvertent. During the Crusades, anemone seed first reached Europe in a pile of dirt from the Holy Land brought back to Pisa and scattered over dead crusaders buried in the Campo Santo. The next spring, the Campo was blanketed with scarlet flowers. Miraculous! The flowers were at once named "blood drops of Christ." Other plants whose seeds were airborne or carried by animals escaped from the gardens into which they had been introduced and became so widespread they were considered weeds. The propagation of most plants introduced from the 17th century on, however, took a lot of effort and was often unsuccessful, since many specimens arrived in Europe in bad condition. Collecting was a chancy business—think of the risk and length of Atlantic crossings under sail—and not much was known about cultivation requirements.

Given the difficulties, what were the reasons for trying to grow these new plants? Scientific, medical, commercial, and aesthetic considerations all played a role. More pertinent to the depiction of gardens in art was the allure of a constantly expanding exotic horizon for the garden maker. Each newly discovered species was recorded by botanical artists, but the plants themselves were only a part of the fun. The wonderful Parc Monceau chinoiserie scene on p. 142 shows the kind of garden foolishness stimulated at home by the introduction of costumes and customs from abroad. Prints of such imaginative new landscapes were widely circulated in garden-making circles. Each vogue in

Not much information about gardens trickled out of China during the early 18th century, and what did seemed too fantastic to be true. Jesuit missionaries reported that the imperial gardens, even larger and grander than Versailles, were laid out irregularly. In 1713 Father Matteo Ripa, an Italian Jesuit at the Chinese court, made thirty etchings of the magnificent garden created in 1703 at the emperor's summer palace outside Jehol. Ripa's prints, from which this one was probably adapted, give little botanical detail. What such views illustrate best is the common European misconception that a Chinese garden was like a landscape park, not a series of "small courts fitted up with rockwork," as the botanist Robert Fortune more accurately reported in 1843.

turn lost its mystery as its plants were naturalized and its culture assimilated. Many plants—tulips, for example—survived novelty to become beloved mainstays of the garden.

Gardens of Cathay

Long after the European vision had faded of Cathay, that mythical land which was the birthplace of chinoiserie, garden pavilions continued to have vaguely Oriental roofs with tipped-up eaves and temple bells. The name Cathay for China dates to Marco Polo's return from Peking in the 13th century, but since the geography of China was unknown for centuries thereafter, extraordinary objects arriving from the East, Indian fabric and Japanese lacquer alike, were described as "from Cathay." So Cathay itself was a hybrid, part Chinese, part Indian, part Japanese, part any strange, uncharted place.

The exotic plants in chinoiserie gardens tended to be North American because few flowers, trees, and shrubs of the Far East were actually introduced into European gardens until the 19th century. But Cathay *did* produce imaginary flowers—fantastic ones—flowers that appeared only in European art and never in gardens. From the beginning of the 17th century, these exotic species sprang up full-blown in painting and tapestry, on porcelain and clothing.

Mantel Clock
Julien Le Roy,
French, c. 1745–49

Julien Le Roy was the most highly
esteemed clockmaker in France
during the reign of Louis XV.
Here Pu-tai Ho-shang, a Chinese
apostle of the Buddha, sits on a
garden bridge. Made in France at
Chantilly, the laughing pagod is
an exact copy of a real Chinese
blanc de chine figure. The little
bridge looks more Rococo than
Chinese, though at this period
bridges "in the Chinese taste"
were being flung across European
garden streams and lakes. The
flowers on the "clock tree" are
standard fantasy flowers of the
period, loosely based on favorites
like the rose and carnation. They
hardly match the exotic looks of
the god himself, or the creatures
(are they silkworms?) that share
the bridge with him.

Plant lore in 16th-century Europe was a mixture of observation and myth. In the foreground of an otherwise perfectly humdrum herb garden stand the mandrake and what could be called the "womandrake." The biforked root of the mandrake (*Mandragora officinarum*), which suggested its human attributes, was used as an aphrodisiac and as a narcotic. The garden includes introduced plants as well as flowers native to Western Europe. The humble lawn daisy (*Bellis perennis*) stands between the mandrake and one of the earliest introduced plants, the Madonna lily (*Lilium candidum*). Accurate information about plant sexuality would have to wait for Linnaeus, about 250 years after the herbal in which this illustration appears was published.

Botanical Adventure

The process of finding real plants, bringing them back alive to Europe, and then experimenting with their culture was arduous and time-consuming, and the results were necessarily slow in evolving. But the difficulties of importation and cultivation alone were not what prevented new species from taking their place at once in the garden landscape. A charming (or not so charming) anthropocentric arrogance was another obstacle. In 1739 the eminent French naturalist Georges-Louis Leclerc, comte de Buffon, wrote of the natural world:

> *Brute nature is hideous and dying; I, and I alone, can render her pleasant and living. Let us drain these marshes, bring to life these stagnant waters, by making them flow. . . . Let us set fire to this useless growth, these old half-decayed forests, then cut away what the fire has not consumed. Soon, in place of the reed and waterlily, from which toads make their poison, we shall see the ranunculus and the trefoil, sweet and healthful herbs. . . . A new Nature will be shaped by our hands.*

Buffon, and many like him, saw the garden as a place for man to demonstrate *his* powers, not nature's. Botanical discoveries, though perhaps beautiful, were strange, maybe even dangerous creatures—best kept in the greenhouse, far away from native plants.

In spite of such conservative warnings, the plants that flooded into Europe from all over the globe eventually reshaped ideas. Plant hunters, naturalists, botanists, and gardeners were increasingly seduced by this "brute nature." Rich

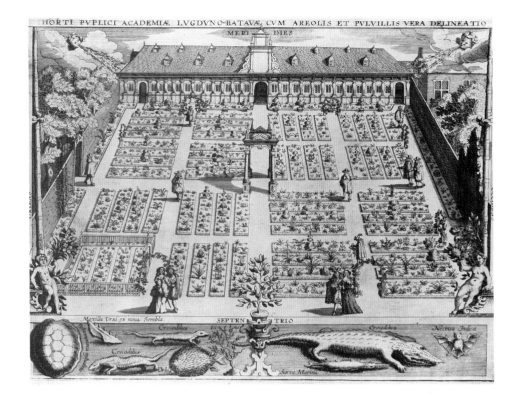

The Leiden Botanical Garden
German, 1655

The collection of unfamiliar plants in the garden is echoed in the collection of strange animals at the bottom of this print from *Hortorum Viridariorumque Formae (The Shapes of Gardens and Pleasure Grounds)*. It must have been almost as difficult for an ordinary gardener of the Renaissance to imagine a tulip growing in his own garden as to think of a crocodile loose in it! Carolus Clusius, director of the Leiden Botanical Garden, introduced the tulip, known as the "Turkish flower," and named after the *tulband*, or turban, to Europe around 1560. *Tulipa clusiana* is still in cultivation; its narrow, graceful white flowers are streaked with wide bands of deep pink.

The Oxford Botanical Garden
Chinese, 1765–1770

This Chinese export plate shows the Danby Gate of the Oxford "Physick" Garden, founded in 1632 and the oldest in Britain. In the foreground stands the garden's first, very eccentric keeper, Jacob Bobart, accompanied by his pet goat. Through the gate we catch a glimpse of the garden, divided into rectangular plots that were kept under lock and key.

amateurs interested in amassing huge plant collections corresponded with explorers and botanists in the field. Funding, both public and private (often from big trading companies like the East India Company or from large commercial nurseries), was readily available for voyages of exploration. Botany became a nationalistic enterprise—the space race, so to speak, of the 18th century. The pride of each country was at stake.

Botanical good fortune rose and fell with the vigor of colonial empires. Spain's share of the booty, which included marigolds and tomatoes from Montezuma's dazzling gardens, dwindled after the 16th century. During the reign of Louis XIV, the power of France abroad was at its height and so was French botanical exploration. As Britain's colonial power and possessions increased, expeditions like that of Sir Joseph Banks and Captain Cook had greater success; by the mid-19th century Britain had taken a clear lead. National botanical institutions in both England and France equipped swift-sailing boats with special equipment to bring plants back in good shape.

The most famous 18th-century collector in Britain was Lord Petre, whose nursery at his death in 1742 contained over 200,000 plants, many of them exotic. Another was the Honorable Charles Greville, known as a collector of women as well as plants. The discoverer of Miss Lyon, later Lady Hamilton and still later Lord Nelson's Emma, he was the first in Britain to bring to flower such supreme beauties as camellias, tree peonies, magnolias, and hibiscus. With the camellia, Greville succeeded where Petre failed. Petre received two wild

Inside a Hothouse (detail)
Alessandro Sanquirico,
Italian, 1829

In the 19th century, conservatories became theaters where dramas of passion and sentiment were played out. Lush, unfamiliar plants and humid warmth made for a languorous—literally steamy—atmosphere where anything could happen. This aquatint shows the design of a stage set for a character ballet. The plants include palms, a gigantic arum lily, cacti, and succulents—the red flowers of the cereus to the far right and the century plant to the left. All the magenta flowers are probably rhododendrons, which were at first thought too tender to put outside. One of the Zouaves is backing up into a prickly pear.

camellias in 1742 and installed them in his hothouse, as was the custom then with all exotics. Since camellias thrive in a temperate climate, the poor things promptly died. Greville had better luck, perhaps because he was the poorer man and not as well equipped.

Petre, Greville, and other aristocratic collectors and gardeners did not have to send out their own ships or depend on amateur collectors for seeds and plants. By the early 18th century professional botanists and plant collectors had a thriving business both at home and abroad. Most interesting of these were two Quakers, Peter Collinson in England and the estimable John Bartram in Colonial Philadelphia. For over thirty years Bartram, a superb naturalist, collected plants and seeds in the swamps, savannahs, and forests of North America from Lake Ontario to Florida, and inland to Tennessee and Alabama. During those thirty years he and Collinson corresponded steadily and sent each other seeds, plants, and complaints about the vicissitudes their precious specimens suffered at sea. To Bartram's collecting efforts we owe many

Design for an Orangery
Salomon de Caus,
French, 1620

This plan for an orangery, a forerunner of the greenhouse, was made by the French engineer Salomon de Caus, who laid out gardens all over Europe in the 16th century. Note the tiny windows, which admit almost no light; for many years it was thought that heat was enough.

Perspective View of the Interior of a Conservatory
Thomas Garner,
British, c. 1800–1820

Conservatories were ideal for romance; throughout their history courting couples would rush to get lost in the shrubbery. Edward VII habitually retired to the conservatory after dinner with the prettiest girl at the party to enjoy two of his greatest pleasures—a big cigar and a discreet feel. It is said that the old ladies hissed at his departure from the drawing room.

Botanic Garden of the State of New-York
After Hugh Reinagle,
American, c. 1816

Dr. David Hosack's Elgin Botanical Garden, one of the earliest in the United States, was established in 1801 on the site of what is now Rockefeller Center in New York City. Exotic plants, such as those grown in this conservatory, were imported into America as well as exported from it. Two plants that now seem native to the South—the camellia (*C. japonica*) and the crape myrtle (*Lagerstroemia indica*)—were both brought to America by André Michaux, botanist to Louis XVI and intrepid plant explorer of North America in the late 18th century.

A calla lily (*C. palustris*) flowers here with two varieties of tender East Indian azaleas, the sort that are still sold today at the florist. The leggy rose may be Maréchal Niel, a favorite of the Victorian conservatory. Such an arrangement of flowering plants, with the tall ones at the back, is reminiscent of the planting in an outdoor border.

beautiful and common American plants, species that really changed the garden: *Magnolia grandiflora*, *Rhododendron maximum*, *Kalmia latifolia* (the East Coast "laurel"), *Pinus Strobus* (the white pine), *Phlox divaricata*—the list is endless. Collinson sent Bartram seeds and plants in return, as well as funding provided by Petre and others for traveling expenses and propagating efforts. Collinson was endearingly greedy for anything Bartram mentioned as a possibility. His letters read like a kind of botanical Christmas list: "Pray send me those Solomon's Seals . . . the great and small Hellebore . . . all sorts of lilies . . . the Devil's Bit . . . any of the Lady's Slipper . . . Black Gum . . . a plant of White Cedar. . . ."

The very science of botany was changed by the influx of new plants. During the fifty years that Philip Miller was Director of the Chelsea Physick Garden in London (1722–71), its holdings grew from 1,000 to 5,000 species. Collinson and Bartram were in constant correspondence with different botanical gardens, European as well as English. Most botanical gardens of the day were affiliated with a university. The first one, at Padua, was set up in 1533 and laid out as a circular area divided into beds for study. It has been said that, while the urge to collect and classify opened up the systematic study of plants in Western Europe for the first time in over a thousand years, it actually retarded garden design. Looking at the monotonously laid out beds in many botanical gardens, one might agree. Both Collinson and Bartram corresponded with Carolus Linnaeus, the Swedish genius who solved the great puzzle of the day—how to classify all these plants and what to call them. Linnaeus's system was simple compared to other systems of the time: he classified plants according to their sexual structure and used just two words to describe each plant. He wanted to dispense with value judgments, such subjective qualities as smell and color, and tried to base the species name on some distinctive part of the plant, often the leaves.

Botany Made Beautiful

Garden design, too, was eventually reshaped by the new discoveries. Throughout the course of the late 18th and early 19th centuries, gardens were transformed from theaters of human society into places to grow and show plants. The hothouse, that horticultural necessity, eventually assumed an ornamental role of its own. Attached to the main house, this building, originally known as a "stove" and inhabited only by gardeners and straight rows of exotic plants, became the elegant conservatory, an indispensable part of the well-laid-out 19th-century pleasure garden.

Most of the new plants required special growing conditions, and this led to the first attempts to make different habitats for different ecological groups, such as alpines, ferns, and water plants. What has been called "Victorian taste" in gardens was partly an enthusiastic popular response to the ever-increasing numbers of plants available. Thorneries, rockeries, heath and rose gardens, and the excoriated plots of annuals or bedding-out plants still seen in public places today were all part of the rush to grow the newest introductions in appropriate habitats.

Throughout the first years of the 19th century, creating these new gardenesque landscapes, heavily planted with flowering shrubs and filled with "features," was easier than one might think. In a sense, the canvas was bare because most flower gardens had been swept away by "th'improving hand" of mid-18th-century English landscape gardeners. As one of Peacock's characters in *Headlong Hall* said disapprovingly: "Your improved places, as you call them, . . . are nothing but big bowling-greens, like sheets of green paper, with a parcel

Basket of Flowers
Eugène Delacroix,
French, 1848

In October 1848, at his house at
Champrosay not far from Paris,
Delacroix hurried to paint this still
life before the first frost. Most of
the flowers are the workhorses of
today's borders, except for the
frightening reddish plant on
the left, love-lies-bleeding
(*Amaranthus caudatus*), happily
not often grown now. The flowers
in the basket include dahlias,
China asters, tithonias, calendulas,
and double African (*Tagetes
erecta*) and single French marigolds (*T. patula*), all introduced
plants. The last two are actually
Mexican, but they arrived in
Europe by different routes. The
flowers in the background,
including the morning-glory-like
climber, are less easily identified.

of round clumps scattered over them like so many spots of ink, flicked at
random out of a pen, and a solitary animal here and there looking as if it were
lost."

North American introductions continued to make their way into the garden
landscape throughout the 18th century. "American gardens" were planted with
American rhododendrons, maples, tulip poplars, and liquidambars. One such
garden is at Painshill in Surrey, where Charles Hamilton, its owner and designer,
was the first to use American plants freely in the landscape. The woods
surrounding de Monville's Désert de Retz outside Paris (p. 69) are still fringed
with shagbark hickories (*Carya ovata*) and other American trees. However,
Greek temples, Chinese pagodas, and rustic hermitages continued to be the
usual garden buildings, since a vogue for Indian wigwams never developed. The
making of romantic, woodsy retreats was spurred on by the spirit of Rousseau's
"noble savage" and the novels of Chateaubriand and Bernardin de Saint-Pierre
about leading the simple life in exotic places.

Following the 1842 Treaty of Nanking, which opened China to the West,
real Chinese and Japanese plants began to arrive in Europe in quantity. Many of
them survived the long trip thanks to the Wardian case, a portable greenhouse
with handles, which works on the same principle as the sealed bottle in which
many schoolchildren have tried to raise ferns. Chinese and Japanese species
changed the general appearance of European gardens greatly, since they
acclimatized as easily as had the North American introductions. Unlike plants

Terrace at Sainte-Adresse
Claude Monet,
French, 1867

Monet's sunny borders could only belong to the 19th century, judging from the central raised bed with its topknot of geraniums (*Pelargonium*), whose double form, seen here, first appeared in 1860. Monet catches a beauty we seldom appreciate today—what better place for the bright colors Victorians loved than against an equally bright ocean? Unlike the gladiolus (*G. gandavensis*) from South Africa, a fairly recent import, the South American nasturtium (*Tropaeolum majus*) ramping along the low wall and climbing the fence was brought to Europe in the 16th century. What was comparatively new in 1867 was the idea of an entire garden of introduced annuals.

from South Africa or Australia, most Far Eastern species came from temperate zones with much the same climate and rainfall as the gardens into which they were introduced. Perhaps this is why they were often used in existing plantings instead of being set aside in new "Chinese" gardens.

South America was the last mysterious land to inspire the creation of a specialized new landscape—the water garden. Naturalist Alexander Humboldt and French botanist Aimé Bonpland made a four-year trip up the Amazon in 1799, bringing back thousands of South American plants, many of them spectacular aquatics. South American introductions continued to arrive in Europe throughout the next hundred years, but the water garden we know, a pond lush with lilies and lotus, did not become widely popular—or possible—in Europe until the late 19th century. Flamboyant plants like the giant Amazonian water lily (*Victoria regia*) popularized the idea of duplicating unusual natural growing conditions. George Lawson, in his book *The Royal Waterlily* (1851), wrote:

The cultivation of exotic plants on the shelves of a greenhouse, however well the specimens are grown, conveys little or no idea of the aspect the

The Morning Ride
James Tissot,
French, 1872–73

By the time Tissot painted his
fragile consumptive model at a spa
somewhere in southern England,
rhododendron and azalea had
been part of the European landscape for more than a hundred
years. The rhododendron she
reaches to touch (maybe for the
last time?) had greatly changed the
look of many large landscape gardens, not always to their advantage. (At Stourhead, one of the
finest mid-18th-century gardens
in England, most of the rhododendrons planted there later are
now being removed.) In time, gardeners learned more than just how
to cultivate these large exotics;
they learned how to make landscapes to suit them. Many beautiful gardens, like Exbury in
England or Biltmore in North
Carolina, were designed to display
rhododendrons and azaleas in all
their glory, just as Tissot captures
them. The azaleas here might be
Ghent hybrids, early *Azalea indica*
crosses that have the tough, sweet-
scented Caucasian azalea, *Rhododendron luteum*, as one parent.

Water Lilies
Baron Adolf de Meyer,
American, 1st half 20th century

Garden historians claim the first
step toward water gardens as we
know them was taken with the
introduction of *Nymphaea
odorata*, the tough American
white-flowered water lily with a
delicious smell. Who can tell what
its reception would have been in
1796 if it had been introduced by
its American nicknames? Europeans swooned over the new lily,
while Americans called it "al-
ligator bonnet" or "water cabbage." De Meyer's limpid
photograph makes the small crystal bowl with two water lilies into
a real water garden.

species present, and the manner in which they are associated in their native
lands; and yet it is avowedly one of the great objects of exotic gardening to
present to the eye vivid pictures of nature, as she is exhibited in the
gorgeous vegetation of tropical lands.

But only with the advent of hardy hybrids such as the water lilies seen in
Monet's painting could the water garden actually move from the conservatory
to the outdoors. Just as it did so, at the turn of the century, other specialized
habitats at last found comfortable places in the new Arts and Crafts garden in
England. With its strong geometry of hedged green rooms, the Arts and Crafts
garden provided a framework sturdy enough to support a fantastic embroidery
of plants from every climate, and its highly defined spaces meant that "vivid
pictures of nature" could exist in the same garden without clashing.

The allure of the unknown sought by 19th-century garden makers, the
sense of strange repose created by the "gorgeous vegetation of tropical lands"
can be felt in Tennyson's incantation, *The Song of the Lotos-Eaters*, published
in 1842. It too is a kind of water garden:

*There is sweet music here that softer falls
Than petals from blown roses on the grass,
Or night-dews on still waters between walls
Of shadowy granite, in a gleaming pass;*

Bridge Over a Pool of Water Lilies
Claude Monet,
French, c. 1890

The first tropical water lily to bloom in the West was probably *Nymphaea capensis*, bright blue, star-shaped, and violet-scented, a South African lily carried back to England on HMS *Gorgon* in 1792. Much water-lily research went on in France, where a great advance was the hybridization of hardy water lilies in luscious tropical colors. Almost all of these hybrids (until well into the 20th century) were the work of Bory Latour-Marliac, a Frenchman who produced his first successful cross in 1879: *N. Marliacea rosea*, pearly pink and still planted today. Monet bought Marliac's sturdy, free-flowering new forms almost as quickly as they became available and introduced them into his gardens at Giverny. He began the water-lily pond in 1893 on a piece of land across the railroad tracks from the main garden. The Japanese-style footbridge, doubtless modeled after a bridge depicted in one of the many Japanese prints Monet owned, follows the axis of the main garden, and acts as a connector between the two parts. Surely no artist has ever made better use of his own garden in his work; in 1899–1900 Monet painted at least seventeen views of the water lilies, and later in life completed another celebrated series as well.

· · · · · · · · · · · · · · · · · ·

Here are cool mosses deep,
And thro' the moss the ivies creep,
And in the stream the long-leaved flowers weep,
And from the craggy ledge the poppy hangs in sleep.

From such langorous music and secret places, the final fruit of so many arduous voyages and such lengthy experimentation, we turn back to the hurly-burly of the kitchen garden.

Working in the Garden

The panel on this red-figure krater—whose unknown painter was named after it—shows a group of women at harvest time. The artist provides an intimate glimpse of the seasonal round in 5th-century Greece; both the pleasures of picking apples and the exertions of carrying a full, heavy basket are depicted with rare naturalism. Orchards lay beyond the city walls, as did the allotments that the common man tilled for food. Such fields were really his garden, since the courtyard of an Athenian house of the period was covered with cobbles or beaten earth.

There are three seasons:
Summer and winter,
And autumn is the third,
And spring is the fourth,
When everything flowers
And nobody has enough
To eat.
> Alkman,
> Greek, 7th century B.C.
> (tr. Guy Davenport)

Long before flower gardens existed, flowers were greeted with joy primarily because they were a sign that food was on the way. Men first gardened to feed themselves: ornamental gardening and the craft of the gardener sprang from agriculture. The Greeks of Alkman's time could doubtless see that flowers were beautiful. They also had the dilemma, still faced by subsistence farmers today, of what to do in spring if the old year's harvest was exhausted: eat the seed grain for next year's crop or go hungry.

The stern necessities of the garden, as a place where food is grown and work is done, tend to be relegated to the borders and backgrounds of works of art. There are some exceptions. Medieval and Renaissance artists depicted the rural occupations of the months and seasons with honesty and in often engaging detail. In the 19th century, manual labor and the daily life of the working class—its dignity and difficulty—again became an accepted subject for artists, with an emphasis on the task in hand rather than on the character of the worker.

Early Working Gardens

Poets and painters have made the pleasure gardens of kings more familiar to us than working gardens, as we should probably call the useful gardens for both vegetables and flowers made before 1700. (Kitchen gardens as such, set aside for

Setting out plants, either vegetable or ornamental, commonly symbolized the start of the growing year. This detail comes from the second of a set of four tapestries in which the seasons and months represent the ages of man. Flowering trees cut into a hedge enclose the garden. The lord of the manor directs operations while three women do the work: one has a rake and a jug of water; another transplants seedlings; and the third sprinkles water from a dish with her fingers. Walafrid Strabo used exactly this method, cautioning that water must be applied on seeds and seedlings "drop by drop lest a too sudden or strong fall of water should move them." The raised beds were also something he used in his own garden:

> Then my small patch was
>   warmed by winds from the
>   south
> And the sun's heat. That it
>   should not be washed away,
> We faced it with planks and
>   raised it in oblong beds
> A little above the level ground.

vegetables and fruit alone, did not develop till around 1750, the day of the landscape garden, when cultivated plots were hidden behind walls away from the house.) How then do we know what these gardens looked like? Surprisingly, early descriptions show us that some kings' gardens were just bigger and more productive versions of average working gardens. Fruitfulness was the true measure of a garden's importance, and even of its beauty. In *The Odyssey* Homer describes the royal garden of Alcinous:

> *Outside the courtyard but stretching close up to the gates, and with a hedge running down on either side, lies a large orchard of four acres, where trees hang their greenery on high, the pear and the pomegranate, the apple with its glossy burden, the sweet fig and the luxuriant olive. . . . In the same enclosure there is a fruitful vineyard. . . . Vegetable beds of various kinds are neatly laid out beyond the farthest row and make a smiling patch of never-failing green.*
>   (tr. E. V. Rieu)

Roman kitchen gardens were filled to bursting with all kinds of vegetables and fruit; in the first century B.C., gardener and writer Columella grew fifteen

Spring
After Marten de Vos,
Flemish, 2nd half 16th century

In the foreground the chatelaine
stands giving instructions. Around
her swirl all the activities traditionally represented for spring and
early summer: setting out seedlings, herbs, and ornamental
plants in the working garden;
sheep shearing in the farmyard;
and the delights of music, dancing,
and love in the pleasure grounds,
where a treehouse stands rather
like a gazebo on stilts. It is interesting to speculate on the actual
size of the kitchen garden for such
a household. There are sixteen
workers—women as well as
men—shown here, including those
in the background going out to
the fields, and just as many mer-
rymakers.

kinds of cabbage alone. Many writers, including Virgil and Cato, wrote about
their simple country gardens, but no visual records of these survive. Described
as mixed gardens of flowers, herbs, and vegetables, they must have been very
different from the elaborate Roman pleasure gardens seen in wall paintings from
Pompeii or Boscoreale.

During the Dark Ages such distinctions were lost. No pleasure gardens
survived the fall of Rome and no one bothered to make any new ones, but the
working garden continued to exist because everyone still had to eat. It is easy to
imagine colorful, scented flowers, notably the rose, lily, and iris, growing next to
the vegetables and medicinal plants. Some techniques, such as grafting, and a
few tools, notably the hand plow and the spade, survived the general loss of
garden lore. In the 9th century, a Benedictine monk called Walafrid Strabo
wrote a practical manual which shows that the gardener's craft has not changed
much from that day to this:

> *If you do not let laziness clog*
> *Your labor, if you do not insult with misguided efforts*
> *The gardener's multifarious wealth, and if you do not*
> *Refuse to harden or dirty your hands in the open air*
> *Or to spread whole baskets of dung on the sun-parched soil—*
> *Then, you may rest assured, your soil will not fail you.*
>   Walafrid Strabo, *Hortulus* (tr. Raef Payne)

Joan of Arc
Jules Bastien-Lepage,
French, 1879

When Bastien-Lepage painted the scene of Joan of Arc listening to her voices at Domrémy in 1425, he chose his parents' garden in Lorraine as a setting. The countryman's garden, serviceable even if untidy, has probably changed little through the centuries. Standard roses and cabbages grow together near the house, and apples ripen overhead. To the right, faggots are piled against a tree to dry, perhaps prefiguring Joan's death at the stake. Weeds are underfoot everywhere, and in the foreground are big brown burrs—a stand of fuller's teasel (*Dipsacus fullonum*)—left on their stalks so that the prickly heads can be used in the cloth-making process. Joan seems to have been winding wool when interrupted by the voices; her frame and overturned stool can be seen behind the teasels.

Of all gardens, the working garden has probably altered less than any other. Untended as it is, Joan of Arc's plot in the 19th-century picture by Bastien-LePage mixes vegetables, flowers, fruit—and weeds—in a way that many contemporary gardeners will doubtless recognize.

As life in the Middle Ages became easier and more affluent, gardeners once again began to develop different kinds of gardens, and artists began to illustrate them more frequently. Given the prevailing taste among artists' clientele for pictures of aristocratic pleasure gardens, it is surprising that so many images exist of practical gardens and gardeners at work. Many of these illustrate the best-known book on medieval gardening, *Opus Ruralium Commodorum* (*The Advantages of Country Living*), also known as *De Agriculture* (until the 17th century the distinction between field work and domestic gardening remained imprecise). Its author, Piero de Crescenzi (1230–c. 1320), a retired Bolognese lawyer, divided his work into twelve chapters, two of which dealt with horticulture. When we consider the flood of new gardening books now published every year, it is a relief to think that the most up-to-date garden book throughout the Middle Ages was always the latest edition of *Opus Ruralium Commodorum*.

Tools of the Trade

Throughout the Renaissance, images of working gardens, and of work in the garden, continued to look much alike. *Spring*, an engraving after de Vos, shows

Woodcutters
Flemish, c. 1500–1525

Woodcutters clear the ground of trees—the first step in making a garden—and put up a fence to enclose pomegranate, pear, and apple trees in fruit. Grazing stags and does indicate that this is a deer park. The tapestry, woven in Tournai, is a reminder that during the Middle Ages and Renaissance much of the arable land of Europe was covered with dense forest. Making a garden in those days was more than a simple matter of planting seed.

Pruning Tools
French, c. 1575–1600

Handles inlaid with mother-of-pearl must have made pruning tasks more pleasant for some 16th-century French gardener. The three beaked knives, or billhooks, were all-purpose tools, widely used implements for pruning trees and shrubs and trimming hedges. The knife and the combined hammer/rasp/file/auger were used for grafting fruit trees, among other things. The saw was used in tree surgery, as it is today, to remove damaged or unwanted branches cleanly. The clippers are the most up to date of all; there is even a socket in the end of one handle so they can be mounted on a pole to get at the otherwise unreachable twig.

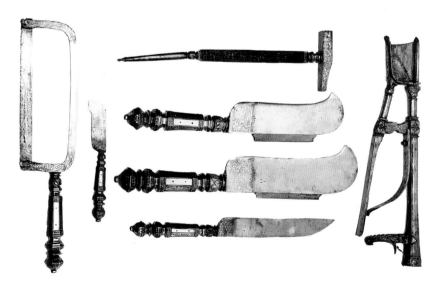

A Gardener (detail)
Attributed to Painter "B,"
Iranian, c. 1525–1530

In the corner of a miniature from
the *Shah-nameh* (Book of Kings)
depicting a marriage celebration, a
gardener with a spade stands by a
stream under a flowering peach.
An old man hands him a little
golden fruit—perhaps a reward
for his labor. The gardener is
dressed for work, with one arm
bared and trousers rolled.

the same activities as the tapestry detail of April from the *Four Ages of Man*. De
Vos even shows Alcinous's grapes, growing up a trellis right next to last winter's
cabbages. But some changes *have* taken place. In de Vos's farmyard is a pair of
turkeys imported from America, at the time much rarer than the peacock staring
at them from the fence. Of interest to the practical gardener is the man digging
with a spade that has a "foot hole." Anyone whose foot has slipped off the top
of a spade, bruising an instep, must wonder why such a contraption has not
survived. Perhaps because the whole blade cannot be used—just half a shovelful
can be dug up at a time. Every other gardening activity and tool shown by de
Vos is the same as today's: we still rake the seed bed to a silky brown carpet,
smooth the earth over new seed with the back of a spade, transplant tender
seedlings we have grown indoors, and hastily prune and tie up big climbers
before they burst into uncontrollable leaf.

The generally unchanging nature of garden tools is surprising. Common
garden tools recorded by artists and still in use today include hoes, mattocks,
rakes, watering cans, and baskets to lug things in. Until the invention of power
tools, only the lawnmower, invented in the 1830s by Edwin Beard Budding, and
the hose were new. An amazing survival is a set of 400-year-old pruning tools
(p. 125). Not only do we recognize them, but Roman gardeners would have too.
The billhooks, still used to pull deadwood down from the tops of trees, are
descendants of the old Roman *falx vinitoria*, or vinedresser's knife. They helped
to make the garden as well as to maintain it, as they were especially efficient in
removing underbrush and vines when land had to be cleared. In a 16th-century
tapestry illustrating the enclosure of a combined orchard and deer park, a
woodcutter uses his billhook to cut and twist green vines, lashing them around
the fencepost.

Once the ground was cleared and plowed, the man with a spade could go
to work. Spades have always been made in a variety of shapes, with pointed,
round, or square ends, depending on the job. The simplest spades were made of
wood, but their cutting edges wore out quickly. When metal was scarce and
expensive, an all-metal blade would have been prohibitive, so the typical
medieval spade, which is still seen occasionally today, had a metal-shod wooden
blade to give it a sharp and durable edge. The 16th-century Iranian gardener
pictured in a miniature from the *Shah-nameh* carries a truly elegant spade over
his shoulder; the tapered metal blade is finished at the handle joint with a
slender neck.

Garden Seeds and Catalogues

Collecting seed is as old as agriculture itself, and plant hybridization is an
ancient science: examples of ancient hybrids that are still extremely useful are
large-kerneled corn developed by the Incas and extra-fluffy Mayan cotton.

Planting Lilies and Leeks
German, 1512

Two woodcuts from a 16th-century Austrian edition of Piero de Crescenzi's *Opus Ruralium Commodorum* show the gardener's round. In one it is autumn, time to plant lilies (probably *Lilium candidum*). The weary *giardinarus*, his metal-shod spade cast at his feet, is perhaps carrying manure to fertilize the lily bulbs. The lily in full bloom no doubt shows what he hopes will grow. At right, a man sets out leeks in a trench he has dug with a mattock. "The tooth of Saturn" is what Walafrid Strabo called the mattock, which he employed to attack nettles in his garden.

The Way They Live
Thomas Anshutz,
American, 1879

Although the tired-looking woman hoeing her cabbage rows was painted after the Civil War, the artist seems to make the point that things are not much better than before. This black family is still living at subsistence level, and the work is hard. The cabin and its cabbage patch are set against a thick background of trees. Hollyhocks are in bloom, and the corn tassels are just visible. Anshutz, a student of Thomas Eakins, was born in Kentucky in 1851 and would have known scenes like this from childhood.

Woman Watering Rosemary
German, 1512

A woodcut from a 1512 German edition of Piero de Crescenzi's *Opus Ruralium Commodorum* shows a tubbed rosemary "tree" being watered from a plain jug not unlike the one carried so carefully by the child in Anshutz's scene of the American South in 1879. The rosemary has been standardized, that is, pruned to a tree shape with a single stem, instead of being allowed to grow in its natural bushy form.

Watering Pot
British, late 15th or early 16th century

This simple orange-brown, glazed earthenware jug has a secret: its base is perforated. When the jug is submerged completely in a fountain or spring, it fills up. The water is retained and its flow regulated by the pressure of a thumb placed over the mouth of the jug. Today, we use a spouted watering can, with or without a "rose," but there is an elegant simplicity to this older method.

The Watering Pot at Work
Flemish, 1592

The watering pots in this illustration from a late 16th-century emblem book have improved in design from the earlier version, with broader bases that sprinkle a wider area. Notice the little rectangular beds stuffed with flowers and the very stout fence and gate complete with lock.

E. J. Bowen Seed Catalogue
E. Wyttenbach,
American, late 19th century

Nurserymen's catalogues and seed packets continue a tradition of gardening vignettes showing the gardener with the hoped-for fruits of his labors. In America, plain brown wrappers came first, though, with the Shakers, who initiated commercial seed sales in "papers," or packets, during the first quarter of the 19th century. Illustrated mail-order catalogues were a big success from their first appearance in the 1830s; chromolithographs like this one followed after the Civil War, and still later, illustrators as well known as N. C. Wyeth and Maxfield Parrish were among those who supplied the art. On the front cover here a man with a hose waters a large, well-tended garden, perhaps a portrait of Bowen's California nursery trial grounds. The vegetable abundance shown above includes asparagus and celery, both of which have been blanched, quite a sophisticated garden practice.

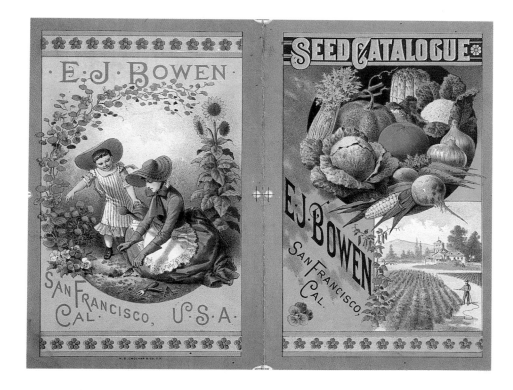

Hybridization has produced many of the flowers and vegetables we love, including Gloriosa daisies and Silver Queen corn, though sometimes it seems that new hybrids are just that—novelties. One American gardener said of the strawberry hybrids created in the 19th century: "There are more berries now than churches; and no one knows what to believe." However, in days before refrigeration and rapid transport, the number of hybrids available extended the season for many vegetables and fruits; twelve kinds of sweet cherries recommended in *The American Home Garden* (1859) ripened from the last of May to the end of August.

Today, information about new seeds and plants customarily travels by catalogue, though seed has long been traded; in prehistoric Britain, Phoenician sailors bartered turnip and radish seed for fox and marten pelts. Botanical institutions, professional plant collectors like the Englishman Peter Collinson, and just plain gardeners traded and sold seed informally, but commercial seed houses did not develop in numbers until the early 19th century. (The first American seed house was Landreth's in Philadelphia, founded in 1784.) Since then, nursery catalogues have been the gardener's winter solace—and temptation; Henry Wadsworth Longfellow pointed out when his spring seed catalogues arrived "that man was first tempted in a garden."

Praying Mantis
Japanese, 19th century

How lightly the praying mantis
steps from a tiny begonia leaf into
the air! Delicate rootlets trail
down from the mother plant in
the hanging container and search
for a foothold, just as the praying
mantis does. This brilliant portrait
of insect and plant is executed in
gold, pewter, and abalone shell on
the lid of a lacquer writing box.

Garden Denizens

We usually share our gardens with many animals. Sometimes, when rabbits or
beetles have been at work, it seems they have rather too large a share. But
people, after all, spend only a few hours at a time in the garden, working or
relaxing, while many garden inhabitants live there all the time. Some perform
indispensable garden tasks: the bee, provider of honey, is vital in pollination;
the praying mantis eats insects that have designs on our vegetables and fruits.
Certain creatures endear themselves to us and so we protect them, even
learning about their life cycles in order to do so. Others we learn about only to
determine the right moment to spray. Because most garden animals are small

Miniature Dovecote
Staffordshire,
British, c. 1750–1770

This ceramic dovecote is one of a pair, its lively modeling set off by the characteristic cream and brown mottled glaze of Whieldon ware. In France during the Renaissance, the size of a dovecote indicated rank and was regulated accordingly—a sort of animal sumptuary law. Doves, besides being good to eat, are useful to the garden because they provide much-prized fertilizer and pest control (although with their love of cabbages and other vegetables they can be pests themselves). They also contribute their soft music and the pattern and splash of wings in the air.

An Earthworm
Jean-Baptiste-Michel Papillon, French, 1755–1759

Only a French Rococo artist could have transformed the humble earthworm, so necessary for soil aeration, into an elegant tailpiece wreathed in single and double roses, hollyhocks, and lilacs. Liberties have been taken with scale, making the worm enormous in proportion to the flowers.

and fast-moving, we are aware of them intermittently and briefly, but occasionally we are transfixed by the beauty or strangeness of what we see. Fortunately, the artist's unwavering eye provides us with what we seldom have in nature: the luxury of a long look.

The Gardener's Trade

An earthworm used as a book decoration and improbably wreathed in flowers evokes the spirit of 18th-century "play gardening"—that supreme unreality of French court life seen at its best in the *fêtes galantes* of Watteau and Fragonard. In the 16th and 17th centuries, gardens were a setting for the performance of masques and fetes. In the 18th century the players jumped out of the masque and performed impromptu for themselves. In art as in life, pretend shepherd-

esses, farmers, dairymaids, and gardeners wandered through romantic landscapes inspired by the works of Claude Lorrain, Nicolas Poussin, and Hubert
Robert.

In the earliest years of the 18th century the gardens—Versailles, Fon-
tainebleau, Marly, Sceaux, and others—were their formal selves, grown older
and shaggier, and for a time pruned a little less severely because royal funds
were temporarily low. With the death of Louis XIV in 1715, the taste for
elaborate but lighthearted informality increased, and gardens were left
deliberately unkempt. Some of the fashionable new gardens inspired by the
English landscape park were *fermes ornées*, a term coined by Philip Southcote,
an Englishman who was the first to carry out the idea of an ornamental farm, or
a farm as garden. The most famous of these was Marie-Antoinette's model
farm, Le Hameau at the Petit Trianon, designed by Hubert Robert.

Meanwhile, the work of maintaining the careful disarray of the new
picturesque gardens was carried on by many hard-working gardeners. The craft

Opposite: *His Highness the Dauphin Plowing*
Michael Wachsmuth,
Swiss, before 1765

In this curious scene, the oldest son of Louis XV plows a field in spring, fertilizing the earth with his touch, so to speak. The plowhorses have been specially caparisoned for the event, and the real plowman in his smock cautiously keeps his hand on the reins.

> O Earth, bare thy breast! Ennobled this day
> Is useful Agriculture, object of our contempt.
> Humanity smiles, and all Nature too,
> To see at work the object of our love.

So runs the accompanying legend in French. Before the end of the century, the French Revolution and the execution of the dauphin's son, Louis XVI, would bring such play-acting to an end.

The Element of Earth
François Boucher,
French, undated

In this charming sketch representing one of the four elements, two children, dressed up to play gardener, assemble a luscious basket of autumn fruits and vegetables. Their Rococo working garden includes a stand of hollyhocks to the right, and what looks very like a pumpkin—that American import—in the foreground.

of the professional gardener grew with the range of exotic plants and the expanded use of greenhouses. Gardening became an increasingly skilled trade. In pictures gardeners are sometimes seen bending over extravagant beds of flowers, shearing hedges, or using their watering cans. No longer are they directed by a watchful owner or chatelaine; other figures seem utterly oblivious to them. We might call them the invisible men, as indeed in life they were often meant to be. Even today people can remember when labor was plentiful before World War I and gardeners were supposed to make themselves scarce. When the owners walked through the gardens, gardeners slipped behind the hedge, or turned to make themselves *very* busy with their work.

Nonetheless, during the many years of the invisible men, a different perception of work and the working classes was developing. Early in the 19th century, the Romantic movement had the effect, in artistic terms, of placing the ordinary man's life and labor closer to center stage. Throughout the century,

Gardener's Certificate
Bohemian, 1780

When under-gardener Anton Schmidl went out to find another job early in 1780, he took this certificate of satisfactory service from his boss, Sebastian Makowetz, "gardener of the pleasure gardens of Ernest Josef Carl, Count Pachta, lord of Zitolieb and Clostrow in Bohemia." Vignettes illustrate the gardener's lore: shearing topiary and hedges; caring for potted shrubs and trees; propagating in the greenhouse; and growing rare and tender plants.

Trimming the Hedge
French School, 17th century

In a typical 17th-century garden, a gardener quietly gets on with his work, shearing a hedge that divides the bosquet from the allée on the right. Trees within the bosquet are "limbed up" (their lower branches removed) so that garden visitors can walk within their shade. The branches that face the allées have been trimmed to a straight line; ladders mounted on rolling platforms were used to get to the tops. Besides looking well to eyes accustomed to formality, such trees do not "shade out" the hedge below, as untrimmed ones would do.

View of the Château de Chantilly
(detail)
Jean Rigaud, French, 1738

Two shirtsleeved figures work among the flowers, one in the stooped posture so hard on a gardener's back, the other using a watering can. In the foreground is an enormous orange tree in a *caisse de Versailles* (the large planters used in all royal gardens). In autumn weather, a hinged side of the *caisse* was dropped down, and the tree in its huge pot was trundled off to the warm orangery.

however, popular sentimentality also developed among many artists and writers
about the past, about childhood, about the simple and the poor, which could be
barbarous in its disregard of the reality of people's lives in "idyllic" rural
surroundings. Some artists, though, managed to avoid sentimentality: Seurat's
Gardener, whose monumentality transcends its tiny size, presents a deeply
convincing image of work. The plein-air painters, especially the Impressionists
and Post-Impressionists, and photographers of the 19th and 20th centuries have
given workers on the land a new identity in portraits that emphasize their
humanity, their struggles, their personalities.

Van Gogh's apple trees, lifting reddened branches to the wet spring sky,
belong to one of the oldest kinds of gardens men know. Despite their wild
looks, they are sweetly familiar, a reminder of the long round of seasonal tasks
and splendors that will always tie gardeners to their land. Van Gogh may have
been reminded of this himself, for he included all the marks of the grower's
care—as well as the unforced and unstoppable beauty of the flowers and young
leaves. We see a rake for the windfalls of the previous autumn that may still lie
on the ground, a scythe to cut the summer grass propped in the crotch of a tree,

Migrant Potato Picker,
Belcross, North Carolina
Jack Delano,
American, 1940s

Photographing for the Farm Se-
curity Administration after the
Great Depression, Delano captured the dignity and difficulty of
life for this man, down on his
knees in the dirt, where the garden
begins and the food we eat is
grown. Until the end of the 17th
century, almost everyone who
worked in the fields had some
kind of a garden, but the separation of agriculture from gardening
and the subsequent specialization
of labor inevitably mean that there
are now many who do not.

A Cottage Garden
Frank Meadows Sutcliffe,
British, first half 20th century

When the camera recorded these
two rural Englishmen at the front
door of a cottage, the scythe had
already been largely replaced by
the mower and the reaper. Sutcliffe was aware that a very old
way of life, and the skills that
accompanied it, were fast disappearing, and he took many photo-
graphs of the workers of Eskdale,
in Yorkshire. This luxuriantly
dishevelled frontage gives us a rare
glimpse of how many cottage gardens must really have looked. The
man with the scythe does not seem
to have been very busy with this
lawn, but the shrubs under the
window and the ostrich ferns on
the left are thriving.

The Flowering Orchard
Vincent van Gogh,
Dutch, 1888

In February 1888, van Gogh left
wintry Paris for Arles, in the south
of France. There, in March and
April, as spring advanced, he
painted fourteen canvases of
flowering fruit trees, of which this
is one. His aim, as he wrote his
brother Theo, was to capture "a
Provençal orchard of outstanding
gaiety." Provençal fruit orchards—apricot, peach, plum,
cherry, pear, and apple—were
often surrounded by a cane fence
like the one seen here in the
distance.

whitewash on the trunks (an old remedy against borers), and string laced
through the branches, probably to keep birds away from both flower and fruit.
The airy, globular shape of these trees is not natural but the result of pruning to
open up the branch structure, admitting air and light that will make for better
fruit. But orchards and kitchen gardens do more than share their fruit with us;
through them we are part of an ancient democracy of gardeners that stretches
back to the apple pickers of the Orchard Painter's krater.

CHAPTER EIGHT

Gardens for the Public

Unlike gardens, parks, those public places we take for granted in cities, arose from commercial needs and from a desire for recreation and amusement. In ancient Greece and Rome, in medieval times, and even in the Renaissance, the most significant gathering places for the population were not gardens at all but squares and markets. Though these may have been ornamented with a little greenery (the Athenian agora did have trees), they were primarily centers for assembly and commerce. There was no great need for recreational green spaces as long as cities were small and the countryside was not difficult to reach. During the Middle Ages, green spaces in cities usually were the grounds of private houses or lay within the precincts of temples and, later, churches. Gardens were places for retreat and contemplation; as a rule they were not open to the public. There were exceptions to private ownership: in 1290 Florence passed a statute setting up a *pratum commune*, or common meadow, and in 1297 an artificial lake was added. The sites of the Prado in Madrid and the Prater in Vienna must also once have been common meadows, judging from their names.

In Italy, the gardens created for the great Renaissance villas were open to a select public and increasingly became places for festivities and spectacles, though again admission was limited to certain classes. In Northern Europe, Antwerp, the capital of Flanders, initiated what could be called the ancestor of the public park. By 1569 the graveyard of the cathedral there had been cleared of tombs, and trees had been planted. The area was called Groenplatz, or Green Square, a name that indicates how unfamiliar the idea of a planted square then was. Renaissance city walls, wider than those of the Middle Ages, provided a place for people to walk and breathe a little fresh air, and Antwerp was the first city to plant these ramparts with trees, a practice that was to catch on throughout Europe. John Evelyn, visiting Antwerp in 1641, commented that "there was nothing about this city which more ravished me than those delicious shades and walks of stately trees, which render the fortified works of the town one of the sweetest places in Europe." In the 19th century ramparts were taken down all over Europe, and many cities were expanded and remodeled to suit the increases in population, traffic, and commerce. Part of the newly available space where the walls had come down was used for green promenades, as at the Ringstrasse in Vienna.

A Bosquet at Versailles:
The Water Theater
Jean Rigaud,
French, c. 1738

Versailles had been designed for crowds long before it went public. Here we see just a few members of the court of Louis XV, together with their dogs, on foot and in the wheeled chairs always available in the gardens, enjoying themselves at the sight of seventy-five fountain jets, which varied their patterns of play four different ways.

Infant Blowing a Conch Shell
French, c. 1670–1680

Imagine this robust lead baby, probably made for one of the bosquets at Versailles, gleaming in a pool beneath the high trees, a plume of water emerging from his shell. He exemplifies the charming conceits devised by Charles Le Brun, first painter to Louis XIV, to complement Lenôtre's austerely grand symmetries.

At the beginning of the 17th century, an Italian game and an Italian queen, both transplanted to Paris, provided the models for another kind of parklike promenade. The game was *pallo a maglio*, or pall mall, a form of croquet played in a long, tree-shaded alley. The alleys—and the word "mall" as the description of a place to promenade—lasted long after the game faded in popularity. The queen was Marie de' Medici who in 1616 commanded that there be an elm-lined triple avenue, the Cours la Reine, beyond the city walls, west of the Tuileries gardens. There, in the late afternoon, high society slowly paraded in coaches before being dropped off at the gate of the Tuileries to walk in the cool of the evening. In imitation, other countries quickly built their own malls and *cours*. But all these places were open only to fashionable society, or to those who wanted to be part of it; the rituals of social recognition, fashion, and power were of limited access. Versailles to its inhabitants was known as *ce pays-ci*, this country, a place set apart. The images of the period freely admit us to the fascinating and luxurious world of *ce pays-ci*.

No Need for a Hat and Sword

The park as we know it today, a green spot in the heart of the city, open to all and the property of all citizens, is a child of revolution, both political and industrial. The French Revolution began in 1789 and was followed by half a century of upheaval, ending with the struggles of the 1840s, less bloody but nonetheless powerful agents of change. Before the Revolution, royal parks and gardens in France, like those of Italian Renaissance villas, had been open to the public, and any decently clothed person—that is to say, with a hat and sword if you were a man—could visit. At Versailles it seems to have been remarkably easy, as hats and swords could even be rented at the entrance. Once the Revolution began, all the royal parks and gardens were opened to the public without any class distinction or dress code.

An Artist Sketching
Jean-Honoré Fragonard,
French, c. 1800

Hidden inside each bosquet, court
strollers found a surprise: in one,
in the 17th century, a labyrinth
concealed thirty-eight painted figures illustrating the fables of La
Fontaine. A century later, a more
informal array of flowers and
vines might have been found billowing up and over trelliswork, as
in Fragonard's beautiful drawing.
Such informality did not come
cheap: when the gardens of Versailles became a public park, a
leaner budget forced the floral
displays in the bosquets to become
less exuberant.

Other great private gardens went public as a result of the French
Revolution. The Parc Monceau was laid out in the 1770s for Louis-Philippe-
Joseph, duc de Chartres, cousin of Louis XVI, and later the duc d'Orléans. A
leader of the liberal party before the Revolution, he joined the revolutionaries
under the name Philippe Egalité, only to be guillotined during the Reign of
Terror in 1793. The richest man in France after the king, this anomalous figure
had a passion for everything English. He imported an English huntsman and a
pack of English hounds, and his garden was laid out *à l'anglais*, though by a
French draughtsman and dramatist, Louis Carrogis, known as Carmontelle.

Monceau: View of the Main Pavilion and the "Jeu de Bague"
After Louis Carrogis,
known as Carmontelle,
French, 1778

In the gardens of Monceau laid out by Carmontelle, a fantastic chinoiserie merry-go-round turns while the riders grab at rings suspended from the pagoda roof. The ladies are steadied on their precarious seats by attendants in Chinese dress.

Bather
Jean-Antoine Houdon,
French , 1782

One of Houdon's loveliest sculptures, the *Bather* was originally offered to Louis XVI. The price seems to have been too high for the king, so the duc d'Orléans, who was married to one of the richest women in Europe, acquired the statue for the gardens of Monceau. Originally part of a Rococo fountain group, she sat in a marble basin with a black attendant, cast in dark lead, who poured water over her from a gilt-bronze ewer. The attendant disappeared during the Revolution, and the *Bather* lost her right leg and left hand; these were restored in the 1850s when the fountain was repaired.

The Parc Monceau
Claude Monet,
French, 1876

In the spring of 1876, Monet set up his easel in the Parc Monceau and captured the final state of the garden in a rosy masterpiece which celebrates a very "English" corner, that is to say, a truly informal and parklike spot. William Robinson, apostle of wild gardens, wrote of it in 1867: "In spring it is radiant with the sweet bloom of early-flowering shrubs and trees, and every bed and bank covered with pansies, Alyssum, Aubrietia, and all the best known of the spring flowers, while thrushes and blackbirds are whistling away as if miles in the country, though it is only a few minutes' walk from the Rue du Faubourg St. Honoré."

The duc d'Orléans's gardener was none other than our Scottish friend William Blaikie, master of the English garden in France. Blaikie did not like what he first saw at Monceau in 1777: "The garden is a confusion of Ruins, temples, etc. crouded one upon another . . . which makes a most singular contrast in so small a compass, the walks Serpenting and turning without taste or reason." At once he set about simplifying Carmontelle's designs, "following the nature of the Ground." The most visible relic of Carmontelle's garden today is the Naumachia—described in 1867 by William Robinson as "a small and not pretty lake, half encircled with round fluted columns." Robinson also mentioned the semitropical plants, such as the 30-foot-tall Abyssinian banana (*Musa ensete*) with its swollen base and giant leaves. It is pleasanter to contemplate the superb shrub in Monet's *Parc Monceau*, a shrub very like an old lilac (perhaps the species *Syringa microphylla*, with its small, soft, almost pink panicles and spicy fragrance). Lilacs are long-lived; this one might even have been planted by Blaikie in the 1780s, a triumphant survivor of revolution and of Second Empire taste.

Vauxhall Gardens
After Thomas Rowlandson,
British, 1785

Sharp black shadows and bright
highlights emphasize the nighttime
feeling of Rowlandson's motley
crowd at Vauxhall. Like most
brilliant caricaturists, he probably
struck close to the mark. Among
those gathered to listen to the
music are many, such as the dandy
in the foreground, who clearly
have other interests.

"A Pretty-Contrived Plantation"

So John Evelyn described the New Spring Gardens at Vauxhall in 1661. The
English took their first step toward a truly public park with the innovation of
pleasure gardens that charged an admission fee. Of these the first and most
celebrated was Vauxhall, a little outside London on the south bank of the
Thames. By the 1750s London had several dozen pleasure gardens of the same
kind. In England the ruling classes were not divided, as they were in France, into
court and city factions, each seeking different pleasures in different places. The
four-month-long sessions of Parliament each year drew noblemen, gentry, mere
squires, and their families from the country to London. They were as eager to
enjoy the delights of town as any Londoner, from the general populace to the
powerful and great. The huge crowds who frequented the pleasure gardens were
a heterogeneous lot of lords and ladies, clergymen, apprentices, prostitutes,
officers of the guard, city merchants, pickpockets, and adventurers. Vauxhall's
amusements were chronicled in prints and celebrated in song.

Vauxhall Sheet Music: "An Invitation to Mira" (detail)
After Hubert Gravelot,
British, 1738

> *Come, Mira, Idol of ye Swains,*
> *(So green ye Sprays, The Sky so*
>   *fine)*
> *To Bow'rs where heav'n-born*
>   *Flora reigns,*
> *& Handel warbles Airs divine:*
> *& Handel war...........bles Airs*
>   *divine.*

Promenades Aériennes
French, 1817

Amusement parks were descendants of the public pleasure gardens that had flourished in Paris in imitation of Vauxhall—one such garden was even named "Wauxhall d'été." Beneath this ancestor of the roller coaster stood a café to refresh those brave enough to dare the 400-foot-long slides. The platform stood 63 feet high.

A Design for Fireworks
British, 1813

Firework displays had been part of royal garden fetes since the 16th century and were also used to mark public occasions such as royal birthdays, famous victories, and marriages of state. They were especially effective set off over water because of the dramatic reflections. As they are today, installations for special firework entertainments were often very elaborate and carefully planned: this pristinely elegant watercolor shows a design probably made for the engagement of Princess Charlotte to William of Orange.

Charlotte's Oak in Windsor Forest
British, 1864

Over 450 years old in 1864, when it was 65 feet in girth, Charlotte's Oak was only one of many trees its age and size in Windsor Forest. Rides radiate from the crossing where it stands—a forest pattern seen as early as the 9th century in the hunting preserve of the bishop of Bologna. This photograph shows Charlotte's Oak "civilized" by the addition of a circular garden seat, and the woods underplanted with tall, broad-leaved evergreens. Many European public parks were once hunting forests and deer parks, just as Windsor was.

The ravishing early days of Vauxhall's existence are described by visitors. In 1663 the gardens were still laid out in squares "enclosed with hedges of gooseberries, within which are roses, beans and asparagus." In May 1667, Samuel Pepys wrote in his diary:

Went by water to Fox Hall [sic] and there walked in Spring Gardens. A great deal of company, the weather and gardens pleasant, and cheap going thither: for a man may go to spend what he will, or nothing at all: all is one. But to hear the nightingale, and other birds, and here fiddles and there a harp, and here a Jew's harp, and there laughing, and there [to see] fine people walking is very diverting.

There were more attractions in the walks and woods than Pepys's nightingale: "The windings and turnings in the little wilderness," writes one observer, "are so intricate that the most experienced mothers have often lost themselves here in looking for their daughters."

Though Vauxhall became less rustic, it remained simple. There were
two main parts: a walk lined with trees, and a grove with a bandstand (built in
1735) surrounded by a crescent of supper boxes, seen on the left of a
Rowlandson print. The expensive supper served in these boxes was a familiar
joke—"its dear potations" and its thin slices of ham. However, the energetic
Jonathan Tyers, manager of Vauxhall, managed to turn even a joke at its
expense into an attraction: the entertainer one evening was an expert carver
who undertook to cover the gardens—eleven acres—with slices from one ham!

The nightly music, the 1,500 lamps in an age when evening usually
implied near-total darkness, the mixed company, the thrill of romance, and, not
least of all, the modest cost (without supper, naturally) were what kept Vauxhall
popular for over two hundred years. By the end of the 18th century it had
become a little frayed, so other attractions were added, such as balloon ascents,
tightrope walkers, jugglers, and nightly fireworks. With Queen Victoria's
accession to the throne in 1837, the open free-and-easy spirit on which pleasure
gardens depended began to vanish. The day of free public parks—and of
teetotalling reformers—had dawned.

The Public Park Movement

The entrepreneurial flair that had led to Vauxhall's success also characterized
the developers of London's leafy residential squares, whose heyday is captured
by Gifford Beal's painting of Mayfair. By the 1790s there were sixteen enclosed
gardens whose use was reserved for the inhabitants of surrounding houses. Such
garden cores became essential to the success of any new residential square. Since
the vogue was to have a house near greenery, land developments that incorpo-

This work by an American folk artist shows another kind of public garden. The Claremont Hotel stood near Bloomingdale Road, now Riverside Drive, looking down at the Hudson River near 124th Street. To judge from contemporary travelers' accounts, few hotels had gardens as fine as this. There are two separate areas: one, an elaborately patterned teardrop with neatly bordered flower beds; the other, a shady garden for strolling, with flowers near the house, a picket fence, some shrubs, and a stand of pines. The larger-than-life-sized "man in the tree" is a mystery; possibly he is a hotel sign. Both gardens are planted with the same tall flowers, including perhaps hollyhocks (*Althea rosea*) and yucca (*Y. gloriosa*), but it is hard to tell. It is easy to see, however, that the teardrop garden, like any 17th-century parterre, was designed to be seen from the windows overlooking it.

rated a square, or better still a park, into the total housing scheme sold better than others. Regent's Park (350 acres), which was open to the general public, was the first large park of this kind, begun in 1811 by architect John Nash.

What were the models for these new ventures? The Georgian spa town of Bath was one, with its crescent terraces and airy views over small, informal parks and over the farmland surrounding the town. Bath in turn looked back to the classic 18th-century private landscape park. The terrace houses of Regent's Park resemble an immense country house, and the park itself looks like a landscape garden. By the 1830s Regent's Park was an aesthetic and commercial success, a model for reformers looking for ways to improve London's working-class districts.

A growing public concern for the effects of the fifty-year-old Industrial Revolution had resulted in a body of legislation (the Factory Act of 1819, the Reform Bill of 1832) which took steps to improve working conditions. Protests about the terrible living environment were also made, and in 1842, not without difficulty, the bill was passed for the creation of London's Victoria Park (193 acres), the first park within easy reach of the East End's hundreds of thousands of inhabitants. London had always had vast royal parks, the remains of hunting preserves. Though these crown properties were open to the public, all were in the fashionable West End.

The first municipal parks were also begun in the 1840s, in the industrial towns of Manchester and Birkenhead, across the Mersey from Liverpool. In Birkenhead, the city park (225 acres) was laid out by Joseph Paxton, designer of the Crystal Palace, as part of the new town. In Manchester, four areas of about 30 acres each, located in the heart of the working-class sections, were purchased by public subscription from every level of society, including the working people themselves. Unlike the new London squares and parks, these areas were clearly designed not only to raise real-estate values, but also to provide a place of rest, recreation, and sport—and perhaps incidentally as an assurance that the poor, drugged on greenery, would not become unmanageably restless.

Each park had places to sit and to walk; playing grounds were designed for badminton, quoits, cricket, archery, and, eventually, football; a fountain provided pure drinking water (unusual at the time); and special buildings offered refreshments. Though perennial flowers and bedding plants proved hardy, only a limited range of trees and shrubs were sturdy enough to survive the heavily polluted industrial atmosphere. Even the plane trees (*Platanus orientalis* and *occidentalis*) that thrive in New York City today did not prosper there. Certain rhododendrons survived, as did white poplar (*Populus alba*), the common elder, both silver and gold-leaved (*Sambucus nigra argentea* and *aurea*), and privet (*Ligustrum vulgare*).

Such a prim and proper era, so many people, so little space—of course these parks were overused and oversupervised. "No games or gymnastics permitted on Sunday" (the one free day of the week) and "No males permitted to intrude upon the play-grounds of the females" were among the rules. The

Central Park—Winter
After John Bachmann,
American, 1865

Looking north over the frozen
lake toward the reservoirs on a
moonlit night, we can see what
pleasures Central Park has afforded to New Yorkers from the
moment it was built. We can also
grasp the scope of Olmsted's genius, as great as Lenôtre's, in
providing magnificently scaled
spaces that easily accommodate
thousands of people. (The rectangular reservoir nearest to us
was filled in 1930.)

Figures at a Fountain
Edward Potthast,
American, c. 1900

Potthast, an American Impressionist, drew much inspiration
from his studio overlooking Central Park. Here, in black conté
crayon, he perfectly captures one
of life's great pleasures—cold
drinking water. Access to fresh
water was an important part of
19th-century urban planning,
since not everyone had running
water at home.

parks of Manchester and Birkenhead sound dreary and crowded, but they were
the first, and from them great things would grow. In 1850 the twenty-year-old
Frederick Law Olmsted, soon to make the greatest city parks of America,
stepped off the boat in Liverpool. He stopped for something to eat at a bakery
in Birkenhead, and as he wrote in 1852, the baker "begged of us not to leave
Birkenhead without seeing their *new park*." Olmsted was deeply impressed, as
much by the baker's pride, "the pride of an OWNER," he said, as by "this
magnificent pleasure ground."

Although Prendergast's interest
was visual organization, not jour-
nalistic accuracy, he conveys a real
sense of Olmsted's great Central
Park innovation: separate paths
for pedestrian, equestrian, and
wheeled traffic. The curves and
patterns in Prendergast's work he
absorbed in France from painters
such as Pierre Bonnard and
Edouard Vuillard, who were concerned with reducing the swirling,
plantlike rhythms of nature to the
two-dimensionality of painting.

Frederick Law Olmsted

We know that parks have rules as surely as gardens have weeds, but, every once
in a while, a great park can give us relief, rest, fun, and the momentary fantasy
of complete freedom celebrated by Cole Porter, who made even the deadly
phrase "municipal park" sing.

> *You can walk on the grass, you can picnic anywhere.*
> *When you ride on the switch-back,*
>   *no one ever takes your fare.*
> *And if you're fond of swimming, there's a pool*
>   *over there,*
> *Where you can go in absolutely stark.*
> *What a nice municipal park!*
>
> *If a lover of flowers, you can pluck them at your ease—*
> *In the zoo you can feed the monkeys anything*
>   *you please—*
> *And if you find it fun to faire l'amour*
>   *beneath the trees,*
> *You don't even have to wait until it's dark.*
> *What a swell municipal park!*
>   from Cole Porter, "What a Nice Municipal Park"

Scene in the Boston Public Garden
Maurice Prendergast,
American, 1899

Twenty-four acres of salt marsh
were drained in 1859 to form the
Public Garden, pride of Boston.
Here, in the city of his childhood,
Prendergast made watercolor
sketches capturing the human
grace, color, and liveliness to
which he was perennially drawn.
The wicker baby carriage creaks,
the baby stares straight ahead
beneath the bright shade, and the
little girl turns in a daydream as
her mother bends down to talk.
For most city children, parks are
the only green places to play.

The skinny rectangle of Central Park, five times as long as it is wide, began in 1857 as "eight hundred acres of unredeemed rock and scrub" at the northern end of New York City. It was, at the time, the largest, most ambitious project of its kind ever conceived. Calvert Vaux, an English architect, designed the romantic buildings, and an Austrian landscape architect and botanist, Ignaz Pilat, put in the original plantings, but it is Frederick Law Olmsted who is remembered as Central Park's creator. The great American urbanologist Lewis Mumford has written: "Olmsted had done something more than design a park, battle with politicians—he resigned at least five times—struggle with insolent and rascally city appointees and protect his fantasies against vandals: he had introduced an idea—the idea of using landscape creatively. By making nature urbane he naturalized the city."

Olmsted believed the value of a park went far beyond concerns of health and pleasure. He saw it as a means to resolve the striking social contradictions of a newly industrialized world. Central Park was to be a place where all classes could exist together in common enjoyment of what he termed "scenery." Scenery would act, he wrote, "in a directly remedial way to enable men to better resist the harmful influences of ordinary town life and to recover what they lose from them." Such ideas were not novel at the time, but Olmsted was utterly singular in the strength of his vision and his determination to carry it out.

It is not Central Park's slightly constricted, picturesque landscape—perhaps the best that could be done with such a site—that makes it unique. Rather it is the magnificent planning, which allows so many activities to take place at once. Completely original are the sunken traverse roads, which permit fast-moving city traffic to cross the park but not to enter it, and the superb network of paths, trails, and roads, glimpsed in Maurice Prendergast's painting of 1903.

How did Olmsted arrive at his vision? He was neither an engineer nor a plantsman; he was an observer, a writer, a lover of landscape from childhood, and most of all a "parkomane." As he put it, "while others gravitated to pictures, architecture, Alps, libraries, high life and low life when travelling, I had gravitated to parks." Surely a deep influence on his work was the pastoral landscape of his childhood in Hartford, Connecticut, a hilly countryside of wide views, broad streams, pastures, and groves of trees cleared of underbrush, with a "browse line" marked by the highest level a cow's head could reach. Being part of New England, Hartford also abounded in massive rocks. In England Olmsted had learned about the multiple requirements of recreation and sport that any city park must answer, and, happily, Central Park represents a compromise. In 1859, after he had been appointed superintendent of Central Park (as yet unbuilt), he returned to England for another look at the royal parks and at Birkenhead. Then he journeyed to France, where he studied the brilliant works of city planner Baron Georges-Eugène Haussman and parks engineer Jean-Charles-Adolphe Alphand. He made eight visits with Alphand to the Bois de Boulogne. (Interestingly, before Olmsted was hired by the Central Park commissioners, Haussman had been considered for the job, as had Joseph Paxton, designer of Birkenhead.)

Prospect Park in Brooklyn was an
easier job for Olmsted and Vaux
than Central Park, thanks to fewer
rocks, fewer political struggles
with corrupt city commissioners,
and the absence of a reservoir
cutting the area in two. Most
important, the partners were able
to adjust Prospect Park's bound-
aries for topographical considerations, and so began with a well-
rounded chunk of land rather than
a strip. Ampler dimensions led to
simpler, longer curves and larger
spaces. In both parks, however,
and in every great city park, there
are places for solitude and reflection. Chase painted his wife soon
after they were married and had
moved to Brooklyn. He reveals an
Impressionist's interest in reflected
light and flickering shadows, but
unlike the French, he retained a
dark-toned palette.

Central Park, for all its amenities, was only Olmsted's first step in a
brilliant career. Brooklyn's Prospect Park is even more beautiful, expansive, and
mysterious, and his comprehensive park system in Boston, carried out by
Charles Eliot, was the first of its kind. That sort of comprehensiveness was
perhaps Olmsted's most valuable contribution; his larger vision had led America
from the isolated urban park to a system of parks that was integral to the design
of a major city.

The Harmony of Colors

The relative merits and charms of parks, French, English, or American, can
happily be debated as long as the sun shines, but surely the most beautiful
images of parks, and of people at rest and at play in them, are those of the
Impressionist and Post-Impressionist painters. Many of them depicted the
ebullient new green spaces of Paris, such as the Bois de Boulogne and the Bois
de Vincennes, devised by the team of Haussman and Alphand. Between 1853
and 1870, the two designers created so many new parks, squares, and
boulevards that it would have been hard for a plein-air painter to avoid them.
As William Robinson noted, "instead of having to go a mile or two to see a
public park or garden, one can scarcely go out of doors without encountering
something green and pleasant to the eye."

What were these marvelous places? When Louis-Napoleon, Napoleon's
nephew, became emperor in 1852, he was determined to make English-style

This oil sketch was presumably painted shortly before mid-August 1884, when Seurat began the final version of his greatest work. An earlier sketch had been made without any figures. In this sense, the artist was not unlike a landscape architect, who creates harmonious spaces knowing later they will be filled with human shapes, dramas, and pleasures. Seurat based his painting technique on Chevreul's color theory, the idea that dots of complementary color, seen from a distance, will blend in the spectator's eye. So English garden designer Gertrude Jekyll was to orchestrate color harmonies in the garden.

La Grande Jatte is a small island in the Seine between Neuilly, which was then one of the outermost suburbs of Paris, and Courbevoie. Parisians on their day off came to the restaurants on the island and enjoyed the grassy west bank. Here Seurat painted, where the long afternoon light cast its shadows.

parks. In exile in England from 1838 to 1840, he had envied London its fashionable parks. He also carried away memories of leafy villas and sunny privacy in the new London suburb of St. John's Wood: he kept a mistress there, as did many affluent Englishmen. Back in Paris, he wasted no time in summoning Haussman, who, with Alphand and the brilliant horticulturalist Pierre Barillet-Deschamps, set about converting the public parks and forests of Paris into models of early 19th-century *jardins anglais*.

These *jardins anglais* differed in their ideas of recreation from British parks, which, after twenty-five years of Victorian morality, bore few vestiges of England's rowdy, fun-loving past. Velvet-green British parks, with some of the most beautiful trees in the world, were devoted to the pleasures of sun, air, promenading, riding, and listening to band music: healthy, improving pleasures, or at least not sinful ones. Refreshment and entertainment were not considered appropriate in these public parks, while French parks were dotted with an abundance of restaurants and cafés. These carried on the pleasure-garden traditions and came to be seen, even by the French themselves, as something slightly raffish and peculiarly "French" according to the bourgeois standards of the 19th century. Contemporary French painters recorded every summery moment with delight, and the world flocked to Paris.

In the 1850s and 1860s, the design of French parks was still essentially that of an English landscape garden, ornamented with simple, unpatterned flower beds and naturalized patches of bulbs. The beds of mixed annuals, perennials, and shrubs, usually heavily pruned roses or lilac, were arranged in colors that shaded into one another—more to our taste now than the beds of a few decades later, which were planted with vivid colors in high contrasts. These earlier schemes were carried out in graded tonal sequences of warm or cool colors, with white flowers used as a link between successive tones. The system of planting was based on the color theories of Michel-Eugène Chevreul, a chemist and director of the Gobelins tapestry works, whose book *Principles of Colors and Their Application to the Arts* had been published in 1839. Chevreul explored the rules of complementary colors and their presumed effect on vision, and his ideas were absorbed by many painters, including Delacroix, Pissarro, Cézanne, Monet, and Seurat. His most important rule dealt with the properties and use of white, a "color" beloved by painter and gardener alike. Gertrude Jekyll, whose work with perennial flower borders in England early in the 20th century was based entirely on Chevreul's theories, says it best: "White is the color of light and makes most things beautiful."

Most things *are* beautiful, seen through the eyes of the Impressionists, which surely accounts for the almost universal popularity of their paintings. Contemporaries of these painters, however, found their works silly and incomprehensible. The idea of parks for the public had also seemed ridiculous at one time. Both painters and park makers had had a vision—they had seen something new and given it shape. The pleasure and harmony of the images created by late 19th-century French painters beautifully transformed the idea of

that gawky new garden, the public park. In fact, works of art continue to help form images for everyone—connoisseur as well as occasional museum-goer—of what parks and gardens look like, and perhaps even how they feel.

When we walk into a garden, we bring with us whatever delights we have seen in garden images: the dark, flower-strewn turf in Giovanni di Paolo's *Paradise*, the silvery shower of George Tice's New Jersey apple tree, a lacquer praying mantis looking for a foothold, or the splash of James Tissot's azaleas flooding down a hill. Our perceptions of what the garden before us looks like are affected by these images and by the emotions they arouse. Indeed, so much of what we consider beautiful in a garden or a park has been made so in our eyes by centuries of art. Memory and allusion augment the pleasures of the present. In turn, what we know of real gardens, their sights and smells, their history, the work and play we enjoy in them, informs and amplifies the marvelous images of all the green and flowery places we glimpse in works of art.

LIST OF ILLUSTRATIONS

Endpapers:

The Gardens of the duc d'Aremberg at Enghien (details)
Romeyn de Hooghe (Dutch, 1645–1708)
The Elisha Whittelsey Collection, The Elisha Whittelsey Fund, 1949, 49.95.677, 678

Half title:

"Résidences d'Eté" from *Les Jardins* by André Vera
Paul Vera (French, 1882–1956)
Published in Paris by Émile-Paul Frères, 1919

Frontispiece:

Wang Hsi-chih Watching Geese (detail)
Ch'ien Hsuan (Chinese, c. 1235–after 1301)
Ink, color, and gold on paper, 9⅛ × 36½ in.
Gift of The Dillon Fund, 1973, 1973.120.6

Page 4.

"Les Petits Jardins" from *Les Jardins* by André Vera
Paul Vera (French, 1882–1956)
Published in Paris by Émile-Paul Frères, 1919

Page 6.

"The Trellis Window, Trentham Hall Gardens..." from *The Gardens of England* by E. A. Brooke
Published in London by T. McLean, 1857
The Elisha Whittelsey Collection, The Elisha Whittelsey Fund, 1965, 65.555.1

Page 8.

Peach Blossom Spring
Fan Ch'i (Chinese, 1616–after 1694)
Ink and color on paper, 6⅝ × 8 in.
The Sackler Collections, Purchase The Sackler Fund, 1969, 69.242.10g

Page 10.

"Bahram Gur Visits the Persian Princess in the Purple Palace in the Sixth Paradise" from *Hasht Behisht* (Eight Paradises) of Amir Khosrow Dihlavi
Attrib. to Manohar (Indian, Mughal, act. late 16th century)
Ink, colors, and gold on paper, 9¾ × 6¼ in.
Gift of Alexander Smith Cochran, 1913, 13.228.33

Page 11.

Garden carpet
Northwest Iranian or Kurdistan, c. 1800
Cotton and wool, 18 ft. 3 in. × 7 ft. 8 in.
Gift of William R. Pickering, 1967, 67.156

Page 12.

Copy of wall painting from the Tomb of Minnahkte
Egyptian, XVIII Dynasty, c. 1475 B.C.
Tempera, 48 × 26¾ in.
Rogers Fund, 1930, 30.4.56

Page 13.

The Western Paradise (detail)
Japanese, c. 1300
Color on silk, overall 78⅛ × 31 in.
The Harry G. C. Packard Collection of Asian Art, Gift of Harry G. C. Packard, and Purchase, Fletcher, Rogers, Harris Brisbane Dick, and Louis V. Bell Funds, Joseph Pulitzer Bequest, and The Annenberg Fund, Inc. Gift, 1975, 1975.268.21

Page 14.

"The Temptation of Adam and Eve" from *Le Bible en Francoiz Historiée . . .*
Published in Paris by Antoine Varard?, c. 1501
Harris Brisbane Dick Fund, 1924, 24.16.1

Page 15.

The Expulsion of Adam and Eve from Paradise
Giovanni di Paolo (Italian, 1403?–1482/3)
Tempera and gold on wood, 17¹⁵⁄₁₆ × 20½ in.
Robert Lehman Collection, 1975, 1975.1.31

Page 16.

The Annunciation
Follower of Rogier van der Weyden (Flemish, 2nd half 15th century)
Tempera and oil on wood, 73¼ × 45¼ in.
Gift of J. Pierpont Morgan, 1917, 17.190.7

Page 17.

Untitled woodcut from *Fior di virtu hystoriato*
Published in Florence by Gianstephano di Carlo da Pauia, 1519
Harris Brisbane Dick Fund, 1925, 25.30.14

Page 18.

Virgin and Child with Angels
Bernaert van Orley (Flemish, c. 1492–1541/2)
Tempera and oil on wood, 33⅝ × 27½ in.
Bequest of Benjamin Altman, 1913, 14.40.632

Page 19.

Ia Orana Maria
Paul Gauguin (French, 1848–1903)
Oil on canvas, 44¾ × 34½ in.
Bequest of Sam A. Lewisohn, 1951, 51.112.2

Page 20.

Paradise
Giovanni di Paolo (Italian, 1403?–1482/3)
Tempera and gold on canvas, transferred from wood, overall 18½ × 16 in.
Rogers Fund, 1906, 06.1046

"A General Plan of the Woods, Parks, and Gardens of Stowe" (detail) from *Stowe Gardens in Buckinghamshire . . . Laid out by Mr. Bridgeman* by Sarah Bridgeman
Jacques Rigaud (French, 1681–1753) and Bernard Baron (French, c. 1700–1762)
Published in London by Thomas Bowles, 1746
Harris Brisbane Dick Fund, 1936, 36.28.15

Page 21.

La Monarchia Latina Triomfante (detail)
After Ludovico Ottavio Burnacini (German, 1636–1707)
Engraving, 11½ × 16½ in.
Harris Brisbane Dick Fund, 1953, 53.600.3581

Page 22.

The Old Plum
Attrib. to Kano Sansetsu (Japanese, 1590–1651)
Ink, color, and gold leaf on paper, 68 × 15 ft. 11½ in.
The Harry G. C. Packard Collection of Asian Art, Gift of Harry G. C. Packard, and Purchase, Fletcher, Rogers, Harris Brisbane Dick, and Louis V. Bell Funds, Joseph Pulitzer Bequest, and The Annenberg Fund, Inc. Gift, 1975, 1975.268.48

Page 23.

Relief from the palace of Assurnasirpal II
Neo-Assyrian, 9th century B.C.
Alabaster, 89¾ × 83 in.
Gift of John D. Rockefeller, Jr., 1932, 32.143.3

Flowering Apple Tree in Middletown, New Jersey
George Tice (American, b. 1938)
Gelatin silver, 10¹³⁄₃₂ × 13⁹⁄₃₂ in.
Gift of Mr. and Mrs. Robert J. Massar, in memory of Lee Witkin, 1984, 1984.1184

Page 24.

Child in Forest
Wynn Bullock (American, 1902–1975)
Gelatin silver, 1951
Gift of Ansel Adams, 1984, 1984.1116.1

Page 25.

Garden of Love (Improvisation Number 27)
Wassily Kandinsky (Russian, 1866–1944)
Oil on canvas, 47⅜ × 55¼ in.
Alfred Stieglitz Collection, 1949, 49.70.1

Page 26.

The Bathing Pool
Hubert Robert (French, 1733–1808)
Oil on canvas, 68¾ × 48¾ in.
Gift of J. Pierpont Morgan, 1917, 17.190.29

Page 28.

Italian Garden
John Singer Sargent (American, 1856–1925)
Watercolor on board, 11½ × 18¼ in.
Gift of Mrs. Francis Ormond, 1950, 50.130.74

Page 29.

"Altra Fontana Piu Sopra All'Antecedente Fontana Rustica . . ." (detail) from *Le Fontane delle ville di Frascati, nel Tusculano . . .*, Part 2
Giovanni Battista Falda (Italian, 1643–1678)
Published in Rome by Gio. Giacomo de Rossi, c. 1665
Harris Brisbane Dick Fund, 1931, 31.67.4

The Cortile del Belvedere
Etienne Dupérac (French, c. 1525–1601)
Engraving, 13 × 18¾ in.
Harris Brisbane Dick Fund, 1941, 41.72

Page 30.

"Desseins du contenus du château de Montargis avec les jardins" from *Le Premier volume des plus excellents bâtiments de France*, 2nd edition
Jacques Androuet du Cerceau the Elder (French, 1510–c. 1584)
Published in Paris, 1607
Harris Brisbane Dick Fund, 1930, 30.32

"A Town Garden" from *Architectura Recreationis*
Engraving after Joseph Furttenbach (German, 1591–1667)
Published in Augsberg by Johann Schultes, 1640
Harris Brisbane Dick Fund, 1939, 39.91.9

Rubens's House and Garden in Antwerp
Franz Harrewijn (Dutch, 1662–after 1732)
Engraving, 13⁵⁄₁₆ × 16¹⁵⁄₁₆ in.
Rogers Fund, 1921, 21.14.9

Page 64.

Man Reading in a Garden
Honoré Daumier (French, 1808–1879)
Watercolor over black chalk,
13 9/16 × 10 5/8 in.
Bequest of Mrs. H. O. Havemeyer,
1929, H. O. Havemeyer Collection,
29.100.199

Page 65.

Figure in Hammock, Florida
John Singer Sargent (American,
1856–1925)
Watercolor, 13 5/8 × 21 in.
Gift of Mrs. Francis Ormond, 1950,
50.130.57

Page 66.

The Audience of the Prince (detail)
French, Beauvais, 1722–1734
Wool, 15 ft. 3 1/4 in. × 10 ft. 3 1/2 in.
Gift of Mrs. J. Insley Blair, 1948, 48.71

Page 68.

Party in the Garden of a Castle (detail)
After David Vinckeboons (Flemish,
1576–1629)
Engraving, 16 × 26 7/8 in.
The Elisha Whittelsey Collection, The
Elisha Whittelsey Fund, 1949,
49.95.2276

"A Gothic Structure" from *Gothic
Architecture Decorated* by Paul Decker
Published in London, 1759
Harris Brisbane Dick Fund, 1930,
30.58.4B

*The World of Emblematics (The Watts
Towers)*
Clarence John Laughlin (American,
1905–1985)
Gelatin silver, 10 7/8 × 13 3/4 in.
David Hunter McAlpin Fund, 1962,
62.549.8

Page 69.

"Vue Perspective de la Colonne" from
Jardins Anglo-Chinois, vol. 13
Published in Paris by George LeRouge,
1785
Harris Brisbane Dick Fund, 1933,
33.28.99–121

"La Maison du Désert de Mr. de
Monville" from *Description des
Nouveaux Jardins de la France et de ses
Anciens Châteaux* by Alexandre de
Laborde
After Constant Bourgeois (French,
1767–1841)
Published in Paris, 1808
The Elisha Whittelsey Collection, The
Elisha Whittelsey Fund, 1964, 64.518

Page 70.

Wall painting from cubiculum of the
villa of P. Fannius Synistor at
Boscoreale
Pompeian, c. 40–30 B.C.
Fresco on plaster, 8 ft. 8 1/2 in. high
Rogers Fund, 1903, 03.14.13

Page 71.

"The Grotto of Narcissus" (detail)
from *Hortus Palatinus . . . Exstructus*
by Salomon de Caus
Published in Frankfurt by Joh. Theod.
de Bry, 1620
The Elisha Whittelsey Collection, The
Elisha Whittelsey Fund, 1949, 49.122

"Gezicht van Dieren . . . van den
Taaras" (detail) from *Praetorium
Dieranum . . . Gulielmo*
Published in Amsterdam by Pieter
Schenck, c. 1700
Harris Brisbane Dick Fund, 1941, 41.45

Page 72.

"Vue de grand rocher à Morfontaine"
from *Description des Nouveaux
Jardins de la France et de ses Anciens
Châteaux* by Alexandre de Laborde
After Constant Bourgeois (French,
1767–1841)
Published in Paris, 1808
The Elisha Whittelsey Collection, The
Elisha Whittelsey Fund, 1964, 64.518

Illustration from *The Gallery of Fashion*
Published in London by N. Heideloff,
1794
The Elisha Whittelsey Collection, The
Elisha Whittelsey Fund, 1950, 50.611.1

Page 73.

Red Friend
Lan Ying (Chinese, 1585–1664)
Ink and colors on paper, 4 ft. 10
in. × 18 5/8 in.
Gift of Mr. and Mrs. Earl Morse, in
honor of Douglas Dillon, 1979,
1979.26

Page 74.

Spanish Fountain
John Singer Sargent (American,
1856–1925)
Watercolor, 20 7/8 × 13 9/16 in.
Purchase, Joseph Pulitzer Bequest,
1915, 15.142.6

Fountain figure
Sculptor close to Donatello (Italian,
act. mid-15th century)
Gilt bronze, 24 1/4 in. high
Purchase, Mrs. Samuel Reed Gift, Gifts
of Thomas Emery and Mrs. Lionel F.
Straus, in memory of her husband, by
exchange, and Louis V. Bell Fund,
1983, 1983.356

Page 76.

*A View of the Cascade &c. in the
Garden of Sir Francis Dashwood, Bart.*
(detail)
After William Hannan (British, act. 1750s)
Etching, 21 1/4 × 14 1/4 in.
Harris Brisbane Dick Fund, 1939, 39.4.3

Page 77.

"Yatsuhashi" from *The Tales of Ise*
(detail)
Japanese, Tosa School, c. 1800
Screen, 39 1/4 in. × 10 ft.
Gift of Dr. and Mrs. Maximilian O.
Goldsmith, 1974, 1974.225.2 (9)

Yatsuhashi
Katsushika Hokusai (Japanese, 1760–1849)
Woodblock print, 9 7/8 × 14 5/16 in.
Rogers Fund, 1922, JP1398

Page 78.

A Circular Maze from *Hortorum
Viridariorumque elegantes . . .*
Reverse copy after Jan Vredemann de
Vries (Flemish?, 1527–1604 or 1623)
Original edition published in Antwerp,
1583
Harris Brisbane Dick Fund, 1928, 28.88.9

"Gezicht van Dieren . . . van den
Tarras" (detail) from *Praetorium
Dieranum . . . Gulielmo*
Published in Amsterdam by Pieter
Schenk, c. 1700
Harris Brisbane Dick Fund, 1941, 41.45

Page 79.

Base for statuette
French or Flemish, early 16th century
Ivory, 5 × 4 3/4 × 3 5/8 in.
The Cloisters Collection, 1955, 55.168

"Common Chinese Fence" and
"Garden Paling" from *Chinese
Architecture, Civil and Ornamental* by
Paul Decker
Published in London, 1759
Harris Brisbane Dick Fund, 1930, 30.58.4a

Page 80.

Priapus and *Flora*
Pietro Bernini (Italian, 1562–1629)
with the assistance of Gian Lorenzo
Bernini (Italian, 1598–1680)
Marble, each 8 ft. high
Lent by St. Mary's Abbey, Delbarton

Page 81.

Le Jardinier
After François Boucher (French,
1703–1770)
Wool and silk, 9 ft. 2 1/2 in. × 6 ft. 1 in.
Gift of Ann Payne Robertson, 1964,
64.145.4

Page 82.

The Triumph of Nature over Art
Pietro da Cortona (Italian, 1596–1669)
Pen and brown ink, brown wash over
black chalk, 7 7/8 × 5 3/4 in.
Rogers Fund, 1960, 61.2.1

Page 83.

Spring
French, Paris, c. 1683
Canvas embroidered with silk, wool,
and metal threads, 13 ft. 8 in. × 9 ft.
Rogers Fund, 1946, 46.43.1

Page 84.

Evening in Spring Hills
Chinese, Sung period, 1150–1250
Ink and color on silk, 9 3/4 × 10 1/4 in.
Promised Gift of John M. Crawford, Jr.,
L. 1984.22.8

Page 86.

"Tree Peony and Quince" from *Garden
Flowers*
Ch'en Shun (Chinese, 1483–1544)
Ink and color, 13 1/8 × 22 3/4 in.
Lent by Douglas Dillon, L. 1981.15.16

Page 87.

Arhat in a Cave
Chinese, Ch'ien-lung period, 1736–1795
Gray and brown nephrite, 12 1/2 in. high
Bequest of Edmund Cogswell
Converse, 1921, 21.175.145

"The Bamboo Bank" (detail) from
Garden of the Unsuccessful Politician
Wen Cheng-ming (Chinese, 1470–1559)
Ink on paper, 10 7/16 × 10 3/4 in.
Gift of Douglas Dillon, 1979,
1979.458.1c

Pages 88–89

View of a Garden Villa (details)
Yüan Chiang (Chinese, act. c. 1680–
c. 1740)
Ink and color on silk, 20 9/16 × 9 ft. 8 in.
Gift of Constance Tang Fong in honor
of her mother, Mrs. P. Y. Tang, 1982,
1982.461

Page 90.

Lotuses on a Summer Evening (detail)
Yün Shou-p'in (Chinese, 1633–1690)
Ink and color on paper, 82 1/4 × 38 3/4 in.
Gift of Marie-Hélène and Guy Weill, in
honor of Professor Wen Fong, 1982,
1982.470

Page 91.

Odes of the State of Pin (detail)
Chinese, Sung period, 1150–1250
Ink on paper, 8 3/8 × 45 ft.
John M. Crawford, Jr. Collection, Gift
of The Dillon Fund, 1982, 1983.459

Page 92.

The Pure Whiteness of Winter (detail)
Hsü Ching (Chinese, act. 1st half 15th
century)
Ink on silk, 58 5/8 × 29 3/4 in.
Purchase, The Dillon Fund Gift, 1982,
1982.1.5

Page 93.

Planting Chrysanthemums (detail)
Lu Chih (Chinese, 1496–1576)
Ink and pale color on paper, 42 × 10 3/4 in.
Lent by Douglas Dillon, L. 1981.15.5

Page 94.

Heian Mansion and Garden
Drawing by Stephen S. Sechrist, III

The Way They Live
Thomas Anshutz (American, 1851–1912)
Oil on canvas, 24 × 17 in.
Morris K. Jesup Fund, 1940, 40.40

Page 128.

Illustration frm *Das Buch von Pflantzung* by Petrus de Crescentiius
Published in Strasbourg, 1512
Harris Brisbane Dick Fund, 1926, 26.100.2

Watering pot
English, late 15th or early 16th century
Red earthenware with transparent splash glaze on part, 12¹/₁₆ in. high
Rogers Fund, 1952, 52.46.1

Illustration from *Io Mercerii I. C. Emblemata*
Published in Bourges, 1592
Harris Brisbane Dick Fund, 1932, 32.8.3

Page 129.

Cover of seed catalogue for E. J. Bowen
Emanuel Wyttenbach (American, act. 19th century)
The Elisha Whittelsey Collection, The Elisha Whittelsey Fund, 1948, 48.120.250

Page 130.

Writing box
Japanese, 19th century
Gold lacquer inlaid with mother of pearl and lead or silver, 1½ × 9¾ × 8 in.
Bequest of Benjamin Altman, 1913, 14.40.838 ab

Page 131.

Dovecote
English, c. 1750–1770
Ceramic, 9½ in. high
Gift of Mrs. Francis P. Garvan, 1940, 40.171.7

Vignette from *Fables de la Fontaine*
Jean-Baptiste-Michel Papillon (French, 1698–1776)
Harris Brisbane Dick Fund, 1932, 32.89.7

Page 132.

Monseigneur le Dauphin labourant
Michael Wachsmuth (Swiss, act. 1760–1770)
Engraving, c. 16 × 21½ in.
The Elisha Whittelsey Collection, The Elisha Whittelsey Fund, 1953, 53.523.57

Page 133.

The Element of Earth: Two Children Gardening
François Boucher (French, 1703–1770)
Charcoal, stumped, a little black chalk, heightened with white on brown paper, 30 × 22⅛ in.
Louis V. Bell Fund, 1964, 64.281.1

Page 134.

Testimonial for Anton Schmidt from Sebastian Makowetz
Bohemian, 1780
Pen and black ink on vellum
Gift of Harry G. Friedman, 1954, 54.633.2

Illustration from *Garden with Alleys*
Published in France, 17th century
The Elisha Whittelsey Collection, The Elisha Whittelsey Fund, 1962, 62.659.46

Veiie du Château de Chantilli prise du Parterre de l'Orangerie (detail)
Jean Rigaud (French, 1700–1754)
Engraving
Harris Brisbane Dick Fund, 1953, 53.600.1211

Page 135.

The Gardener
Georges Seurat (French, 1859–1891)
Oil on wood, 6¼ × 9¾ in.
Bequest of Miss Adelaide Milton de Groot (1876–1967), 1967, 67.187.102

Page 136.

Migrant Potato Picker
Jack Delano (America, b. 1914)
Gelatin silver
The Elisha Whittelsey Collection, The Elisha Whittelsey Fund, 1972, 1972.741.8

Two Elderly Men
Frank Meadows Sutcliffe (British, 1853–1940/41)
Gelatin silver
David Hunter McAlpin Fund, 1967, 67.541.46

Page 137.

The Flowering Orchard
Vincent van Gogh (Dutch, 1853–1890)
Oil on canvas, 28½ × 21 in.
The Mr. and Mrs. Henry Ittleson, Jr. Purchase Fund, 1956, 56.13

Page 138.

Panorama: The Palace and Gardens of Versailles (detail)
John Vanderlyn (American, 1775–1852)
Oil on canvas, c. 12 ft. × c. 165 ft.
Gift of Senate House Association, Kingston, N.Y., 1952, 52.184

Page 140.

"Le Théâtre d'Eau" (detail) from *Vues des bosquets du jardin de Versailles*
Jean Rigaud (French, 1700–1754)
Engraving
Harris Brisbane Dick Fund, 1953, 53.600.1279

Infant Blowing a Conch Shell
French, 1670–1680
Lead, 23 × 43½ in.
Purchase, Josephine Bay Paul and C. Michael Paul Foundation, Inc. Gift, and Charles Ulrick and Josephine Bay Foundation, Inc. Gift, 1969, 69.78

Page 141.

Le Dessinateur
Jean-Honoré Fragonard (French, 1732–1806)
Black chalk, 10¼ × 10⅞ in.
Robert Lehman Collection, 1975, 1975.1.626

Page 142.

Vue du principal Pavillon du jeu de Bague
After Louis Carrogis, known as Carmontelle (French, 1717–1806)
Engraving published in Paris, 1778
Harris Brisbane Dick Fund, 1942, 42.412

Bather
Jean-Antoine Houdon (French, 1741–1828)
Marble, 47 in. high
Bequest of Benjamin Altman, 1913, 14.40.673

Page 143.

The Parc Monceau
Claude Monet (French, 1840–1926)
Oil on canvas, 23½ × 32½ in.
Bequest of Loula D. Lasker, New York City, 1961, 59.206

Page 144.

Vaux-Hall
After Thomas Rowlandson (British, 1757–1827)
Engraving and aquatint, 21 × 30 in.
The Elisha Whittelsey Collection, The Elisha Whittelsey Fund, 1959, 59.533.975

Page 145.

The Invitation to Mira, Requesting Her Company to Vaux Hall Garden
After Hubert Gravelot (French, 1699–1773)
Musical broadsheet, 1738
Harris Brisbane Dick Fund, 1946, 46.33

"Promenades Aeriènnes" from *Observations sur les Modes et les Usages de Paris*, known as Bon Genre
Published in Paris, 1817
Harris Brisbane Dick Fund, 1938, 38.38.5

Bridge Illustrated with Fireworks Celebrating a Royal Marriage
British School, 1813
Watercolor, 14⅜ × 23¼ in.
The Elisha Whittelsey Collection, The Elisha Whittelsey Fund, 1963, 63.607.1

Page 146.

"Charlotte's Oak" from *The History of Windsor Great Park . . .* by William Menzies
Published in London by Longman Green, 1864
The Elisha Whittelsey Collection, The Elisha Whittelsey Fund, 1973, 1973.519.1

Page 147.

Mayfair
Gifford Beal (American, 1879–1956)
Oil on canvas, 28 × 25⅛ in.
Arthur Hoppock Hearn Fund, 1914, 14.72

Page 148.

The Claremont
American, 19th century
Oil on canvas, 25½ × 34 in.
The Edward W. C. Arnold Collection of New York Prints, Maps, and Pictures, Bequest of Edward W. C. Arnold, 1954, 54.90.169

Page 150.

Central Park—Winter
After John Bachmann (American, 1826–1909)
Color lithograph, 13¼ × 19⁵/₁₆ in.
Harris Brisbane Dick Fund, 1947, 47.53.10

Figures at a Fountain
Edward Potthast (American, 1857–1927)
Black conté crayon, 22 × 29½ in.
Gift of Mr. and Mrs. Raymond J. Horowitz, 1969, 69.154

Page 151.

Central Park in 1903
Maurice Prendergast (American, 1859–1924)
Oil on canvas, 20¾ × 27 in.
George A. Hearn Fund, 1950, 50.25

Page 152.

Page 29 from *Large Boston Public Garden Sketchbook*
Maurice Prendergast (American, 1859–1924)
Watercolor on paper, 14¼ × 11¼ in.
Robert Lehman Collection, 1975, 1975.1.952

Page 153.

Mrs. Chase in Prospect Park
William Merritt Chase (American, 1849–1916)
Oil on wood, 13¾ × 19⅝ in.
The Chester Dale Collection, Bequest of Chester Dale, 1962, 63.138.2

Page 155.

Study for A Sunday on La Grande Jatte
Georges Seurat (French, 1859–1891)
Oil on canvas, 27¾ × 41 in.
Bequest of Sam A. Lewisohn, 1951, 51.112.6